THE
UNWRITTEN
ORDER

THE
UNWRITTEN
ORDER

HITLER'S ROLE IN
THE FINAL SOLUTION

PETER LONGERICH

TEMPUS

First published 2001
This edition published 2003

Tempus Publishing Limited
The Mill, Brimscombe Port,
Stroud, Gloucestershire, GL5 2QG
www.tempus-publishing.com

© Peter Longerich, 2001, 2003

The right of Peter Longerich to be identified as the Author
of this work has been asserted in accordance with the
Copyrights, Designs and Patents Act 1988.

British Library Cataloguing in Publication Data.
A catalogue record for this book is available from the British Library.

ISBN 0 7524 2564 1

Typesetting and origination by Tempus Publishing Limited
Printed in Great Britain by Midway Colour Print, Wiltshire

CONTENTS

The German Regime in Poland

PREFACE

At the end of 1997 I received an unusual request. My colleague Richard Evans, Professor of Modern History at Cambridge University and Fellow of Gonville and Caius College, and Anthony Julius, of the London law firm of Mishcon de Reya, asked if I would be prepared to appear as an expert witness in the forthcoming civil action of Irving *v.* Lipstadt.

The background to this spectacular civil action is well known and need not be repeated here in much detail: David Irving, the author of several books on the Nazi period and the Second World War, had begun proceedings against Professor Deborah Lipstadt, Professor at Emory University Atlanta, because in her book, *Denying the Holocaust*, she charged him with having deliberately falsified the history of the Nazi period, in particular by denying the murder of the Jews and Hitler's responsibility for it.[1] In response, Deborah Lipstadt and her publishers Penguin Books decided not only to take up Irving's challenge and face the charge, but also to take the offensive in their conduct of the case. In other words, they resolved to subject Irving's methods to detailed scrutiny before the court and make them the true object of the trial. As part of this strategy, the defence called on a number of historians, who were to demonstrate to the court just how untenable was Irving's attempt to cast into question substantial aspects of the history of the murder of the European Jews that are generally accepted. The goal that the defence set itself was reached: as is also well known, the trial ended in April 2000 with Irving's total defeat.

For the action of Irving *v.* Lipstadt the historians who had been engaged as expert witnesses prepared written reports, some of them very extensive. In the main submission, Richard Evans dealt in detail with 'David Irving, Hitler and Holocaust Denial', but there were four further specialist submissions: a study of the history of the construction of Auschwitz by Robert-Jan van Pelt, an architectural historian teaching in Canada; a study by America's leading Holocaust expert Christopher Browning on the source materials available on the subject of the 'final solution'; and my own two expert reports, the first on 'The Systematic Character of National Socialist Policy for the Annihilation of the Jews', the second on 'Hitler's Role in the Persecution of the Jews by the National Socialist Regime'.

The two reports prepared by me were therefore concerned with two central elements of the history of the murder of the European Jews that have repeatedly been challenged by Holocaust deniers, namely the fact that the murder of the European Jews was the result of the systematic implementation of a specific policy, and the fact that this policy was pursued by the highest authority of the Third Reich, Adolf Hitler. It was not the purpose of either report to deal with Irving's absurd theses (which were to be refuted expertly and in detail by Richard Evans's report); but to explain the current state of research on the events that we call the 'Holocaust'. These considerations also lie at the root of the present undertaking to publish the report elucidating Hitler's role in the 'final solution' in an extended form.

At the point when I took on the commission to write a report on Hitler's role in the persecution of the Jews, I anticipated that the experience of appearing as an expert witness in a British court would be highly interesting but did not expect any great insights to emerge from the writing itself. Seen from an academic perspective, the topic 'Hitler and the Holocaust' seemed unattractive for two main reasons. Firstly, however much historians may debate the genesis of the 'final solution', they are all agreed that Hitler played a central role in the annihilation of the Jews. The way in which he fulfilled this role may be disputed, but the fact that he played a role is not regarded by specialists as a problem that is academically particularly interesting or difficult to solve.

The desire of so-called revisionists like David Irving to deny Hitler's central role in the murder of the European Jews – despite his well-documented vituperative anti-Semitism and despite his unfettered freedom of action as omnipotent dictator – may be of real interest to political historians, psychologists and the like. But to a historian it is clear that this form of argument relies on simple sleight of hand. The starting-point is the fact that an unambiguous written order from Hitler for the murder of the European Jews does not exist (and may well never have existed). The argument that the so-called revisionists develop from this fact is trivial and misleading: it rests on the spurious suggestion that one can derive from the absence of a historical document a negative conclusion about events; what is not documented is therefore non-existent.

Historians are familiar with this classic trap from their training. There is even a specialist term for it, the *argumentum ex silentio*, or the fallacy of deriving far-reaching conclusions about what happened (or did not happen) in history from the absence of documentary evidence.

On the other hand – and this is the second reason why I was initially not particularly interested in the topic of 'Hitler and the Holocaust' – the fact that Hitler played a decisive role in developing the policy for murdering the Jews offers only a very limited explanation for the full extent of what happened. After decades of intensive study of the history of the National Socialist dictatorship, it is perfectly clear that Hitler was the driving force and constant stimulus for radicalising the persecution of the Jews. In this area of policy he had considerable room for manoeuvre, which he employed exactly as he saw fit. Nowadays the vast majority of historians who are concerned with the history of the Third Reich would subscribe to the theory 'no Holocaust without Hitler'. Or, to argue counterfactually, if Hitler had died in 1940, it is extremely questionable whether the Nazi regime would have followed that fateful path under different leadership, or whether the indubitably destructive energy of the system would have been expended in a different direction. But what does the phrase 'no Holocaust without Hitler' actually explain? Seen in purely logical terms it denotes a necessary but not a sufficient condition, so the phrase 'no Holocaust without Hitler' cannot be reversed to give the thesis 'the Holocaust took place merely because Hitler willed it'. For the historical event of the Holocaust to occur, a whole series of other conditions had to be fulfilled alongside 'Hitler', and these conditions had to merge into a historical process that produced the event.

In fact contemporary scholars are working intensively on identifying explanations for the historical events that we now generally term 'the Holocaust'. Amongst the questions that interest modern historians is the question as to the motivation and mentality of the perpetrators, above all of the functionaries in the SS and the Police, and in the German civil administration in the occupied countries. They are also concerned just as intensively with the problem of the stance taken by the traditional elite groups towards the so-called 'Jewish question' and with how far they participated in the genocide – this includes the Generals, the various branches of bureaucracy, the medical profession, scientists and scholars in a wide variety of disciplines (including historians), amongst other groups.

In addition studies are being undertaken into the persecution of Jews at regional level, looking at the question of how far local official bodies possessed room for manoeuvre in anti-Jewish policy, and focusing on the relationship between 'centre' and 'periphery'. Scholarship is also keenly interested in how much the general German population knew about the Holocaust and how it reacted, in the question of whether there was a particularly radical form of anti-Semitism in Germany, and if so, what the historical conditions were that led to it.

Research is slowly clarifying the link between the persecution of the Jews and other areas of National Socialist policy, such as nutrition, the use of foreign workers, the occupation of other countries and policies relating to the relocation of millions of people. Gradually we are reaching an understanding of how the development of policy towards the Jews was influenced by these other areas, and, in reverse, how the 'Jewish question' influenced these areas, too. This list of the important topics of contemporary historical research could easily be extended, but even a truncated account shows clearly how any attempt to claim that the murder of the European Jews could be reduced exclusively or even primarily to the factor of Hitler himself would be wrong-headed.

However, the more I worked on the subject of 'Hitler and the Holocaust', the more my initial lack of enthusiasm for it grew into keen interest – again for two reasons. The first of these is essentially practical in its nature, but has broader implications. Whilst I was preparing the expert witness report, it turned out to be more difficult than I had imagined to assemble the key documents relating to this epochal crime. One might have imagined that a scholar interested in the process of decision-making leading to the 'final solution' could turn to a well-ordered repository of central documents – perhaps even to a printed version of the key documents comparable to an edition of diplomatic papers or a collection of cabinet minutes – yet this is by no means the case here. The documents relating to the murder of the European Jews are dispersed in archives literally all over the world. Publication has only been partial and in so disparate a manner that only specialists are really in a position even to locate such published documents in a reasonable length of time. This is all the more regrettable because the opening of Eastern European archives in recent years has led to the discovery of a whole series of new sources for the subject, which are only gradually being published, again often in very obscure places.

This unsatisfactory situation made the compilation of a report based almost exclusively on original documents preserved in the most varied of archives far and wide a particular challenge. The hearing was to show the great importance of documents from the period in the reconstruction of the historical events by the court. It proved to be the case that most of the questions under debate could only be settled by a precise examination of the relevant documents and often hours were spent in discussion about the authenticity, dating, original authorship, translation and interpretation of individual papers. In some cases it was even necessary to have documents faxed during the hearing from the relevant archives in various countries – an impressive demonstration of some of the gaps in the documentation of the Holocaust that remain to be closed, especially when one keeps in mind the possibilities of electronic communications.

The purely practical challenge that arose from this situation naturally gave rise to the question of why an event with the historical significance of the Holocaust is so comparatively badly documented. It also highlighted the question of the discrepancy between this lamentable state of affairs and the high degree of attention that this topic has attracted in the media, in politics and in the efforts being made for a culture of remembrance. For me, this discrepancy was one of the most significant experiences of the London hearings.

As well as this apparently practical aspect of my work, there was a methodological question closely related to the problems of sources that concerned me as I was compiling my report. This was the question of how best to demonstrate the central role of Hitler in the context of the 'final solution' and, above all, once Hitler's key role had been proved, what conclusions could be drawn from it, less in relation to the man himself than in relation to how we should assess the so-called Jewish policy of the regime and its historical significance.

Historiography has produced two classic methods of dealing with the problem of the Führer's missing order for the 'final solution'. The first approach consists of the attempt to reconstruct the apparently lost order from other documents, fragments and other indications – in other words, to fix a date and a place for when and where such an order must in all probability have been issued. The second method is more structurally oriented and stresses the gradual or incremental

nature of the events: it is assumed that the 'final solution' did
not result from a single order given by Hitler, and what is
stressed is the destructive inherent momentum of the machinery of persecution and annihilation once it had been set in
motion. The 'cumulative radicalisation' (Hans Mommsen) of
the whole process gives only secondary importance to the
question of whether and in what way the dictator was himself involved. This is not to say, however, that the historians
who take this view question Hitler's responsibility for the
whole process.

Nevertheless, on the basis of my own research I had chosen
a different approach. I was not concerned with looking for a
single order issued by Hitler; neither did I wish to work from
the idea that Hitler's involvement in the murder of the Jews
was solely implicit and to be supposed only on the grounds
of his position within the Nazi system and of his well-known
anti-Semitic stance. Instead, I set myself the task of demonstrating via documentary evidence Hitler's almost continuous
involvement with this issue, the task therefore of collecting
the many individual decisions made with regard to the 'Jewish
question', and of establishing from these an overall picture of
a policy that was pursued logically and consistently. At the
same time, I intended to explain, at least in outline, the central role of this anti-Jewish policy in the history of National
Socialism and to show the general context for the gradual
radicalisation of the persecution of the Jews in the various
phases of the development of the National Socialist regime.

If Hitler as an individual stands at the centre of this, it is
not intended to attribute the murder of the European Jews
directly to the single human being, if that is the right word,
but to depict Hitler as a decisive exponent of this policy.
Besides the systematic and comprehensive manner of its

execution, what is special and so far historically unique about this crime is the will to totally annihilate that drove its perpetrators, a murderous intention that was expressed over and over again, internally and in public speeches, by the leader of the Nazi Party, the head of state and commander of the armed forces. It is the fact that the perpetrators saw themselves as legitimised by the authority of their Führer and were prepared on the basis of this authority to commit a crime of unparalleled magnitude that must serve as the decisive point of departure for any explanation of the historical events – not an account that is restricted to the personal activity of Hitler himself.

Whilst the fact that the anti-Jewish policy was continually given sanction and impetus by the regime's highest authority does not offer a complete explanation for this policy, it does make clear its central importance for National Socialism. The 'removal' of the Jews, in whatever manner, the comprehensive 'clearing' of Jews from German society, was the fundamental basis on which the National Socialists intended to erect a racially homogeneous 'community of the people', and at the same time it became the key means of enforcing their rule, first in Germany, later in Europe.

The key role played by Hitler in the decision-making process towards the 'final solution' and the fact that as the 'Jewish policy' was gradually radicalised the protagonists repeatedly appealed to his authority, both of these articulate the central role of the persecution of the Jews in National Socialist politics as a whole. And this is, of course, the reason why Holocaust deniers so stubbornly challenge Hitler's central role in the genocide.

The literature dealing with the causes, the historical conditions and the background for the National Socialists' murder of the European Jews is quite vast, and cannot be summarised here in anything like adequate detail.[2] Hitler's role in this process has naturally been stressed by the so-called intentionalist school, with the object of making Hitler's hatred of the Jews the sole, or at least the main, explanation for what occurred. In this context one might cite authors such as Helmut Krausnick, Klaus Hildebrand or Philippe Burrin,[3] but above all mention should be made of the British historian Gerald Fleming, who, twenty years ago, collected and gave a concentrated analysis of the documents then available on Hitler's central role in the 'final solution'.[4] On the other hand, despite being more interested in structures and processes than in the individual role of the dictator, the functionalist school has made important contributions to his personal involvement. This is especially true of the moderate functionalists, represented best by Christopher Browning, but is also the case for one of the more radical representatives of this school, Martin Broszat.[5] Finally, it is important to make special mention of Ian Kershaw's massive biography of the dictator, which contains the most recent comprehensive depiction of Hitler's role in the National Socialist persecution of the Jews.[6] My own contribution to this topic is *Politik der Vernichtung* (*The Policy of Annihilation*), which appeared in 1998.[7] It formed the basis of the report compiled for the court case and also, therefore, of its publication here in book form.

The original report on Hitler's role in the persecution of the Jews was significantly expanded for the purposes of this publication. I have taken the liberty of incorporating large portions of the second report into the text: the nature of the argument links both expert reports closely together and it seemed sensible to move away from the two-stranded form that was determined only by the preparations for the court

case and to combine both texts once more. Above all, intensive work on the topic of the murder of the European Jews
during preparations for the case and during the trial itself led
to a collaborative exchange of views amongst those involved
that is in some aspects still continuing and has encouraged
me to expand the text in various places.

For this, and for co-operation of an exceptionally high
order during the trial, I should like to thank in particular my
fellow expert witnesses: Richard Evans, Christopher
Browning and Robert Jan van Pelt, as well as Hajo Funke
(who as a political scientist shed light on Irving's radical right-
wing connections in Germany). I should also like to thank
the Defence's research assistants: Tobias Jersak, Nick
Wachsmann and Thomas Skelton-Robinson, and Deborah
Lipstadt's legal team. Alongside the collaboration with
Anthony Julius, Mark Bateman and James Libson, my intensive discussions with Richard Rampton (who as Queen's
Counsel represented Deborah Lipstadt in court) count
amongst the most interesting experiences of the whole trial.
As an experienced lawyer, he succeeded time and again in
surprising the experts with astute observations, unconven-
tional conclusions and fascinating hypotheses on the history
of the Nazi persecution of the Jews, and in making us con-
sider further.

I should also like to thank the directors and staff of the
archives whose holdings were consulted during the compila-
tion of the reports: the President of the Bundesarchiv,
Hartmut Weber, the Director of the Zentrale Stelle zur
Aufklärung von NS-Verbrechen in Ludwigsburg, Willi
Dressen, and the Archivist at the Institut für Zeitgeschichte in
Munich, Klaus Lankheit. During the trial itself, they were all
prepared to supply urgently required documents from their

holdings at short notice, sometimes within hours. That, too, was a unique experience.

Finally, I should like to thank my colleagues and students in the German Department at Royal Holloway, University of London, for their forbearance throughout the period of the trial.

Peter Longerich
Richmond upon Thames and Munich
June 2001

1

REMOVE, ANNIHILATE, EXTIRPATE

Hitler's Anti-Semitic Language

There can be no doubt that Hitler's behaviour throughout his political career – from the end of the First World War until the end of the Second World War – was characterised by radical anti-Semitism. In one way or another, Hitler wished to put an end to the existence of Jews within the 'living space' (*Lebensraum*) of the German people, and this objective carried a very high priority in his political practice.

Of course Hitler's anti-Semitic stance cannot by itself explain the persecution and murder of the European Jews by the Nazi regime. A history of the 'final solution' must nevertheless take account of his central role in the decision-making process, not least because Hitler's constant authorisation and legitimisation of this policy articulated the central importance of persecuting the Jews for National Socialist policies as a whole.

An account of Hitler's role in the genesis of the 'final solution' is complicated by the fact that the dictator avoided the use of explicit written directives relating to the murder of the Jews, and only issued oral instructions on the subject to a single individual or in front of a small group of people. When he did speak about the subject, he used formulations that certainly left room for interpretation or deliberately concealed the true state of affairs. Hitler's behaviour in this respect was initially determined by the desire for secrecy. The murder of the European Jews was treated as classified information by the organs of the Third Reich on principle, which is to say

that no public discussion of the topic whatsoever was permitted.[1] As Himmler said in his speech to the SS elite in
Posen in October 1943, it was 'an unwritten, never-to-be-
written page of glory in our history'.[2]

The official silence on the topic of the 'final solution' did
not prevent leading representatives of the regime from indi-
cating in public, repeatedly, if in very general terms, that the
Jews of Europe were moving towards their downfall or
destruction – which, as we shall see later, is what Hitler in
1939 had announced would happen in the case of a world
war.[3]

However, it was not only the aspect of secrecy, inconsis-
tently practised as it was, that made Hitler and other leading
National Socialists follow the official policy and not speak
openly about the murder of the Jews even when amongst
themselves or in small groups, leading them to disguise their
references to it. This behaviour was doubtless also partly governed by the refusal to take in the reality of the murder of
millions of people. By speaking abstractly of 'annihilation',
they kept the horror of it at a distance. It was forbidden to
refer in any way to the fate of the Jews in Hitler's immediate
surroundings, in his entourage and in front of his guests.[4]
Such denial of reality and self-deception became increasingly
characteristic of the atmosphere in Hitler's headquarters.

The fact that the murder of the European Jews was linguis-
tically obscured in this way makes interpreting the relevant
key documents particularly challenging. The difficulty of this
task is considerably increased by the tendency of the key words
used by the National Socialists in describing the objectives of
their anti-Jewish policy to change their meaning over the years
as the persecution of the Jews became more and more radical.
From mid-1941 onwards, and increasingly from the spring of

1942, Hitler and other leading National Socialists used words such as 'annihilation' (*Vernichtung*), 'extirpation' (*Ausrottung*), 'final solution' (*Endlösung*), 'removal' (*Entfernung*), 'resettlement' (*Umsiedlung*) or 'evacuation' (*Evakuierung*) as terms to camouflage the mass murder of the Jews. In the period before this, they used the same terms with reference to the Jews but without necessarily implying a programme of mass murder. And when they are applied to other ethnic groups, the same terms may have a quite different meaning.

When interpreting the meaning of these terms, therefore, it is important to take into account the various phases of the National Socialists' anti-Jewish policy. They have no meaning independent of the time factor. During the 1920s and as far as the mid-1930s, the main aim of Nazi anti-Jewish policy was to undermine the legal and economic situation of the German Jews so as to force them to emigrate. The Jews were to disappear from German public life and later on, disappear from German territory altogether. When the Nazis used the term 'annihilation' (*Vernichtung*) during these early years, they referred on the one hand to the planned destruction of the allegedly dominant position of the Jewish minority in German society. On the other hand, however, from the context of the relevant texts it is obvious that at this point the term already had a violent and even murderous component to its meaning, however vaguely defined this might have been. In a cautious interpretation, it would not be an exaggeration to describe the meaning of the term 'annihilation' in this early phase as ambiguous. The perspective of mass murder was already present. By way of a summary one is compelled to say that during this period (from the early 1920s to the mid-1930s), the Nazis envisaged as the final goal of their Jewish policy, as the 'final solution', a potentially violent 'removal' (*Entfernung*) of the Jews from German public life and eventually also from German soil.

At the end of the 1930s, the Nazis intensified the pressure for emigration or expulsion. During this period, terms like 'removal' (*Entfernung*) or 'final solution' (*Endlösung*) indicated that the continued existence of a Jewish minority in Germany was no longer possible. The violent aspect of anti-Jewish policy became more and more significant. In the last year before the outbreak of the Second World War the term 'annihilation' (*Vernichtung*) pointed clearly to the possibility of genocide.

Between the outbreak of war in summer 1939 and the middle of 1941, the Nazis were looking for a so-called 'territorial solution' to the 'Jewish problem', that is, they were planning to deport the Jews to territories on the periphery of their empire where there were insufficient means to subsist and where they would inevitably perish. Technically the terms 'resettlement' (*Umsiedlung*) or 'evacuation' (*Evakuierung*) still denoted the idea of the geographical relocation of a mass of people, but one must not fail to note that this vocabulary increasingly incorporated the perspective of the physical end of the Jews in Europe. In this period the term 'final solution' was used in the same way.

Between the summer of 1941 and the spring of 1942 the meaning of these terms changed. They were now increasingly used as synonyms for mass murder. However, even in this period (particularly between autumn 1941 and spring 1942), the terminology can in some cases still be ambivalent. For an accurate interpretation each phrase has to be analysed in its historical context. In particular, in a period in which one Jewish minority after another was being included in the process of systematic mass murder, one has to determine which Jewish minority was indicated by each of the relevant phrases. For example, one cannot exclude the possibility that, in April or even May 1942, i.e. at a point when preparations for the systematic murder of European Jews were well underway, Hitler and the leading organisers of the murder-programme might occasionally have talked about 'alternative' plans for a 'final solution'.[5] It is quite possible, even at this stage, that they may have been referring on certain occasions, in conversation, to earlier plans to deport the European Jews to an area on the outskirts of the German-controlled territories, where they would be killed or allowed to perish. This is especially plausible if such conversations were concerned with the Western European Jews, who in summer 1942 had not yet been officially included in the programme of systematic murder.

The occasional mention of 'alternatives' can be interpreted as reluctance on the part of Hitler and other members of the leading circle of Nazis to articulate openly the true consequences of the decision to kill millions of people, a decision which at this point had already been made and implemented.

2

COMPLETE REMOVAL
OF THE JEWS

Hitler's Statements on the 'Jewish Question'
During the Rise of the NSDAP (1919-1932)

Scholarly opinion is divided on when precisely Hitler became an anti-Semite. The widely accepted suggestion that he had already developed his hatred of the Jews during the Vienna years (1907–13) looks plausible at first sight, but it cannot be documented satisfactorily. It is impossible, for example, to reconstruct what he was reading during his youth, and the fact that in *Mein Kampf* Hitler himself attributes his anti-Semitic 'awakening' to experiences he had undergone in Vienna tends to arouse rather than to allay suspicion. It seems perfectly plausible that Hitler wished to reinterpret retrospectively a dull and difficult period in which he was living from day to day, a failure as an artist and incapable of making a decision about which direction his life should take. The reader of *Mein Kampf* is supposed to see the Viennese years of 'apprenticeship and suffering' as a time of renunciation, a period of heroic attempts to better himself, when the author uses his bitter experience of life as a way of developing his unshakeable ideological principles. But it is no more possible to prove Hitler's assertions in *Mein Kampf* that since then he had refined his anti-Semitic stance during the periods of convalescence and the leave that he spent in Germany in the years 1916, 1917 and 1918.

It is indeed highly probable that Hitler became susceptible to anti-Jewish influences during his time in Vienna – which was one of the main centres of European anti-Semitism – and it is equally credible that he was influenced in the second half of the war by the sharp rise of anti-Semitism in Germany:

but even if such a predisposition is plausible, it is only from 1918, during his stay in Munich and under the influence of defeat, revolution and the rule of Socialist workers' councils, that it is possible to prove how it intensified to become a programmatic anti-Semitic ideology.[1]

The anti-Semitic stance that Hitler finally adopted in the transitional period of 1918-19 is clearly not an isolated circumstance but has to be seen in its context as a mass phenomenon. Anti-Semitism had received a sharp boost from 1916 onwards, but from about the middle of 1919 it is possible to detect a further increase in hostility to Jews in Germany. After the true consequences of the German defeat had come to light in Versailles, after the revolution had been put down with violence and republican forces were on the defensive, there was talk of a 'wave from the right', whose most important indicator was anti-Semitism.

A brief explanation of this phenomenon may chiefly be sought in the fact that significant parts of the radical political Right were now coming to the fore. Anti-Semitic tendencies from the radical Right had repeatedly been making themselves heard since the end of the 1870s, and now they were staking their decisive breakthrough on the anti-Semitism card. After the collapse of the authoritarian Wilhelmine state in 1918, the radical Right began to look closely at its 'ethnic' (*völkisch*) roots. It was believed that a reminder of the virtues and values that were supposedly slumbering deep within the German people would achieve a total renewal of 'Germanness', from below, from the level of the people itself. It turned out, however, that this search for identity was best realised negatively, by distinguishing a German identity from a sector of the population that had for centuries been the object of hatred and scorn: the Jewish minority, who were largely assimilated and in any case represented less than one per cent of the total population. From then on, the political Right made 'the Jews' responsible for well-nigh every glitch in the development of Germany – for revolution and defeat, for Socialism, for economic difficulties, for the harsh conditions imposed by the Treaty of Versailles, for the decline of tradition and moral values, and more. Being 'liberated' from the Jews, on the other hand, meant redemption from the greatest evils. With the help of anti-Semitism, the radical Right had not only created a dominant new political agenda, it had produced something akin to a negative identity.

The upsurge in anti-Semitism was not only manifested in the founding of large numbers of anti-Semitic organisations, although these were very significant, too: the largest of them, the Deutschvölkische Schutz- und Trutzbund (German League for Protection and Resistance) had more than 100,000 members and possessed considerable propaganda resources. This upsurge was evident, too, in the adoption in April 1920 of anti-Semitic thinking into the programme of the German National People's Party, the political union of the German conservatives. It was noted that Jews had emerged to play leading roles in the revolutionary period, and that the Republic was now represented by Jewish politicians, and this took on central importance in the climate of anti-Semitic agitation. Hitler's early anti-Semitic statements, which will now be considered in more detail, were therefore perfectly in tune with a strong element in the zeitgeist.[2]

Hitler's very first political statement, his letter to Adolf Gemlich of 16 September 1919, already includes a clear declaration of his anti-Semitic position. Gemlich had taken part in a programme of political education to which Private Hitler had been assigned as an instructor in summer 1919, his oratorical talent having attracted the attention of his superiors. Such programmes were intended as a means of immunising soldiers who were about to be demobilised against dangerous revolutionary ideas. Hitler's tuition had already displayed a strong anti-Semitic tendency, so strong, in fact, that the officer responsible for the course in his training camp had warned that him he should moderate his views. Four weeks after the end of the course, on 16 September 1919, Hitler wrote to Gemlich on behalf of Captain Karl Mayr, who had been responsible for the course syllabus:

Anti-Semitism of the purely emotional sort finds its ultimate expression in the form of pogroms. Rational anti-Semitism, on the other hand, must lead to the systematic judicial opposition to, and elimination of, the privileges which the Jews hold in contrast to the other aliens living amongst us (special legislation for aliens). Its ultimate unalterable objective must be the removal of the Jews altogether.[3]

This attitude is constant throughout all Hitler's early public statements on the issue. Almost all his speeches contain anti-Semitic passages;[4] time and time again he demanded the 'removal' (*Entfernung*) of the Jews from Germany.[5] The radical nature of his statements at this point is remarkable: as early as 1920 he was speaking of 'extirpation' (*ausrotten*) and 'annihilation' (*vernichten*). Thus, according to a police report of a NSDAP meeting on 6 April 1920, he declared:

We have no intention of being emotional anti-Semites intent on creating the atmosphere of a pogrom; instead, our hearts are filled with an inexorable determination to attack the evil at its core and to extirpate it root and branch. In order to

achieve our goal every means will be justified, even if we have
to make a pact with the devil.[6]

In a speech to a meeting of National Socialists in Salzburg on
7 August 1920, he said:

> Do not imagine that you can combat a sickness without killing
> what causes it, without annihilating the germ; and do not
> think that you can combat racial tuberculosis without taking
> care to free the people from the germ that causes racial tuber-
> culosis. The effects of Judaism will never wane and the
> poisoning of the people will never end until the cause, the
> Jews, are removed from our midst.[7]

It can be demonstrated that Hitler used the words 'remove'
(*entfernen*) and 'annihilate' (*vernichten*) synonymously. In a letter
to a sympathiser, headed 3 July 1920, he wrote:

> I cannot reproach a tuberculosis bacillus for doing something
> that means destruction for a human being but life for the
> bacillus itself; I am no less compelled and legitimated in
> conducting the battle against tuberculosis by annihilating [*ver-*
> *nichten*] its cause, because my very existence depends on it.
> Over thousands of years, the Jew is becoming and has become
> a racial tuberculosis affecting many peoples. To fight him
> means to remove [*entfernen*] him.[8]

Hitler left no room for doubt that the ultimate goal of
National Socialist Jewish policy could only be attained by
using violence. In a speech made in April 1921 he shouted:

For this reason solving the Jewish question is the central question for National Socialists. This question cannot be solved delicately; faced with the terrifying weapons of our opponents, we can only solve it by using brute force. The only serious way of fighting is fighting hard. Lord Fisher said, 'if you strike, then strike hard! The only serious fight is one that makes your opponent scream.'[9]

Hitler's involvement in drawing up the NSDAP party programme in 1920 was decisive. Amongst other things, this programme called for the removal of German citizenship from the Jews and their treatment under 'special legislation for aliens'. As early as 1922 Hitler made a public speech in which he demanded the death penalty for 'any Jew caught with a blond girl'.[10] In January 1923, in Munich, he promised,

There is no possibility of accommodation here: the Jew and his accomplices will forever remain enemies in the hearts of our people. We know that when they take the helm, our heads will roll; we also know, however, that when we have power in our hands, God have mercy on you![11]

In his book *Mein Kampf*, which appeared in 1926, and especially in a manuscript written in 1928 that remained unpublished until after 1945 (his 'Second Book'), Hitler put his radical views about 'removing' the Jews from Germany in the context of a theory for which he tried to find a historical derivation.[12] According to this theory, the meaning of world history is a permanent struggle between races or peoples for 'living space' (*Lebensraum*). In this model the Jews, whose particular racial disposition is said to prevent their developing their own territorial state or culture, play the role of parasitic

beings, acting together with other Jews in an international conspiracy, who seek to destroy from within the
construction of empires of *Lebensraum* by superior races. Hitler
describes this 'theory' most clearly in a lengthy section of his
'Second Book':

> Because they lack their own productive capacity, the Jewish
> people are incapable of establishing their own state territori-
> ally. Rather they need the work and creative capacity of other
> nations as a basis for their own existence. The very existence
> of the Jews thus becomes parasitic on the lives of other peo-
> ples. The ultimate goal of the Jewish struggle for survival is
> therefore the enslavement of productive peoples. To achieve
> this goal, which in reality represented the struggle for exis-
> tence of Jewry in all ages, the Jew makes use of all weapons
> that correspond to the whole complex of his being. On the
> domestic level, he fights within individual nations initially for
> equality, and then for superiority. The weapons he uses for
> this are cunning, cleverness, subterfuge, malice, dissimulation,
> etc., qualities that are rooted in the very essence of his ethnic
> character. They are ruses in his struggle for survival, like the
> ruses used by other peoples in combat by sword.
>
> On the level of foreign policy he attempts to make nations
> restless, distracting them from their true interests, propelling
> them into internecine wars. In this way, with the help of the
> power of money and of propaganda, he attempts to impose
> himself on them as their master. His ultimate goal is 'de-
> nationalisation', the promiscuous bastardisation of other
> peoples, the lowering of the racial standards of the best; at
> the same time he aims at gaining mastery over this racial hotch-
> potch through the extirpation [*Ausrottung*] of the native
> intelligentsia and its replacement by members of his own people.

The end of the Jews' struggle for world domination will therefore always be bloody Bolshevism, which in truth is the destruction of the intellectual elite that derives intimately from the essence of a nation, with the result that he can ascend and make himself master of a mankind rendered leaderless. Stupidity, cowardice and wickedness play into his hands. It is in the bastard that he secures for himself the first opening that will enable him to break into the body of another people.

The end of Jewish domination is always the decay of all forms of culture, finally even the insanity of the Jew himself. For he is a parasite on a nation and his victory signifies his own end as well as the death of his victim.[13]

As *Mein Kampf* and his 'Second Book' clearly demonstrate, Hitler perceived the situation of Germany after the end of the First World War as the consequence of an international Jewish conspiracy: Jews dominated both 'international finance capital' and the Socialist movement, they were responsible for war, revolutions, the decline of national values and for the pernicious 'mixing of the races'.

The language that Hitler used in this early period to refer to the Jews was filled with boundless hatred. Eberhard Jäckel once compiled a series of typical designations for Jews from *Mein Kampf*: 'like a maggot in a rotting corpse', 'a pestilence worse than the Black Death', 'a germ-carrier of the foulest kind', 'mankind's eternal bacterium', 'the spider began to suck the blood of the people slowly out of its veins', 'a pack of rats fighting bloodily among themselves', 'a parasite in the body of other peoples', 'a sponger radiating further and further like a harmful bacillus', 'the eternal bloodsucker', 'a parasite on the people' and 'vampire'.[14]

An analysis of Hitler's public pronouncements in the second half of the 1920s clearly shows that anti-Semitism was continuing to play a central role in his thinking. In Hitler's speeches from that time hatred of the Jews was by no means a marginal element used only for purely demagogic purposes. Rather anti-Semitism was the central component of the ideological structure that he endeavoured to convey to his listeners with stubborn perseverance.

For even if Hitler was *primarily* concerned in his public utterances in the second half of the 1920s with the political questions of the day, in the great majority of his speeches and articles he would return to the ideological trains of thought that he had developed in *Mein Kampf* and his 'Second Book'. For him these were the explanation of the precarious situation in which Germany found itself at the end of the First World War.

Central categories in Hitler's public statements thus continued to be 'space' and 'race': the future of the Germans as a racially superior people depended, he said, on their being in control of as great a space as possible.[15] The fulfilment of this historical mission, which, according to Hitler's central argument, was decisive for the security of the existence of the German people, was obstructed by systematic attempts on the part of the 'Jewish race' to prevent it.

Over and over again, Hitler repeated in his speeches his stereotypical grievances against the Jews: he said that they were not able to work productively and were incapable of creating culture;[16] that they lacked a positive attitude towards the soil; that instead they had others work for them and gained interest from them.[17] He therefore called the Jews 'parasites' or 'spongers' (*Schmarotzer*).[18] In Hitler's view their cunning activities had enabled them to gain control of the economy.[19]

Despite themselves being incapable of producing culture, they had been able to dominate the culture industry and the press, and therefore controlled public opinion.[20]

In addition, the political parties were in his view dominated by the Jews.[21] This was especially true of the Socialist parties.[22] In a characteristic statement he called Marxism the 'great instrument for the annihilation of the Aryan peoples, for the annihilation of the intelligence of these Aryan peoples and for the constitution of a thin Jewish upper class'.[23] In the Soviet Union he felt that this goal had already been largely achieved through Stalin's dictatorship.[24]

On an international level, too, the Jews were said to have achieved a dominating position in the economy: he claimed that 'international finance Jewry' used their position to put additional economic and political pressure upon Germany.[25] Communism and capitalism were, in Hitler's view, both instruments in the hands of Jews for the attainment of a position of world domination: 'Western democracy on the one hand and Russian Bolshevism on the other are the forms in which the present Jewish world conspiracy finds its expression.'[26] The international order created by the Versailles Treaty was an instrument by which the Jews could annihilate the German people.[27]

In Hitler's view, the Jews had thus largely succeeded in infiltrating, manipulating and dividing the German people. The Jews were responsible for the fact that the German people had already begun to turn away from the task that was decisive for their future – that of accumulating soil and working it.[28] The inner dividedness of Germany, the political conflict between the bourgeoisie and the workers, was also the work of the Jews.[29] In his speeches, Hitler frequently used the metaphor of a 'body of the people' (*Volkskörper*)

penetrated by a foreign germ in order to describe the supposed dominant position of the Jews within the German
'Volk',[30] or that of a 'cancer' to be removed.[31]

This chain of reasoning led Hitler to the conclusion that
Germany's problems could only be solved properly by elim-
inating the supposed dominance of the Jews. He developed
specific concrete suggestions for achieving this that were
entirely based upon the Party programme of the NSDAP.
These involved the elimination of the economic ascendancy
of the Jews and – in the event that they should not submit
to this – their physical removal: 'If he conducts himself well
then he can stay, if not then out with him!'[32] Hitler also prepared his listeners for the concept that this settlement of
accounts with the Jewish mortal enemy would not be an
easy task, but might involve a difficult and, if necessary, violent confrontation.[33]

If one considers the function of anti-Semitism within
Hitler's thinking, it becomes clear that it played the role of
the central binding element in a hotch-potch of highly con-
tradictory ideas. Hitler's public statements in the second half
of the 1920s make it clear that his world-view was incon-
ceivable without his anti-Semitism. He promised his listeners
that once the 'Jewish problem' was dealt with, he could solve
Germany's basic dilemmas in the areas of foreign and domes-
tic policy, as well as in the economic, social and cultural realms.

After 1930, when the NSDAP had become a party with a
mass appeal, the anti-Semitic element began to recede
markedly. Clearly Hitler was aware of the fact that the number
of those voting for him had surpassed the number of radical
anti-Semites in the German population.[34] A more precise
analysis of his speeches reveals however that he had not in any
way altered his basic ideology.

In the years 1930–33, too, when the NSDAP attained unprecedented electoral success, the basic elements of Hitler's ideology – 'space' and 'race' – remained at the centre of his speeches.[35] On various different occasions, Hitler stressed that he continued to regard the 'Jewish race' as the main enemy of the German people. Thus in a speech in Munich made on 29 August 1930, a few days before the greatest electoral victory of the Nazis in the Reichstag elections, he stated with regard to the Jews, 'the head of another race sits upon the body of our people [*Volkskörper*]; the heart and the head of our people are no longer one and the same.'[36] In another speech a few weeks later, he portrayed the struggle against the Jews (without naming them) as a divinely appointed task:

> When we as German try to protect ourselves against being poisoned by another people, then we are trying to return into the hands of the almighty Creator the very same essence that he has bestowed on us.[37]

Thus, even if the anti-Semitic elements in Hitler's rhetoric were reduced after 1930, the 'Jewish Question' had clearly by no means given up its central position in his ideological world-view. He and the leadership of the NSDAP continued to proceed on the premise that the solution to this 'problem' would give them the key to shaping the decisive questions that concerned Germany's future. From their perspective, however, making Germany 'free from Jews' was also the crucial step towards gaining complete power in the land.

3

ERADICATION FROM THE CULTURAL AND INTELLECTUAL LIFE OF THE NATION

The Beginnings of Anti-Jewish Policies (1933)

An overview of the National Socialists' persecution of the Jews between 1933 and 1939 reveals that there were three clearly distinct phases. Whilst in 1933 and 1934 the displacement of the Jews from public life was a central political ambition, from 1935 the policy pursued by the Nazi regime was one of segregation and of comprehensive legal discrimination against the German Jews. It was in autumn 1937 that the last and most radical phase of anti-Jewish policies was initiated: the German Jews were then completely stripped of their judicial rights; the gradual process of expropriating Jewish wealth that had been begun as early as 1933 was rapidly brought to its conclusion in a formally legalised manner; and above all, the expulsion of the Jews that had so long been the aim of National Socialist policy was now pressed forward with the threat and the use of force.

In all three phases the escalation of the persecution of the Jews was initiated by acts of anti-Semitic violence by Party grass-roots activists, who were at each stage 'brought into line' after a relatively short period by the organs of Party and state – on Hitler's explicit instructions. The National Socialist leadership reacted to the violence of spring 1933 with the official boycott of Jewish businesses of 1 April 1933 and a first series of anti-Semitic laws; the renewed anti-Semitic disturbances of spring and summer 1935 were followed-up in the Nuremberg laws; the violence of 1938 that culminated in the so-called 'Night of the Broken Glass' (Kristallnacht) was followed by a veritable flood of anti-Semitic legislation. From 1933 to 1939, therefore, there developed an interaction between National Socialist supporters and the National Socialist leadership that was to prove typical of the Nazis' persecution of the Jews – a sophisticated co-operation between activism 'from below' and formal measures 'from above'.

What role did Hitler play in this process? Were his anti-Jewish measures primarily a reaction to the demands of the Party activists, or were the actions of the grass-roots members of the Party one component of a scenario that he had carefully designed, part of a targeted policy?

The first phase of anti-Semitic policies began immediately after the Reichstag elections of 5 March 1933 when the National Socialists and their conservative coalition partners gained the majority of the votes (albeit by illegal means). As early as 7 March National Socialist Party activists launched a wave of anti-Semitic violence in various areas of Germany. They daubed and barricaded Jewish businesses, and in many towns forced their way into court buildings in order to prevent Jewish lawyers from exercising their profession; furthermore, in several cases they attacked and assaulted Jewish citizens.

However, it would be completely wrong to assume that it was this wave of anti-Semitic violence on the part of Party members that put pressure on Hitler and the National Socialist leadership to initiate a deliberate and consistent policy of anti-Semitism. The reverse is true: the leadership always had the flood of anti-Semitic violence under control. On 10 March Hitler called for a halt to Party activists' 'individual actions' that were hindering the work of the authorities or interfering with businesses owned by Jews or others.[1] And the anti-Jewish violence did indeed come to a stop after a few days. An attack on the Reichsgericht in Leipzig, Germany's highest court, that had been planned for March by the local Party organisation was cancelled on Hitler's personal instructions.[2]

So at the end of March, when the Nazi leadership changed its political line, a not inconsiderable propaganda effort was needed to spur on the Party activists once more to a large-scale boycott of Jewish businesses. In this first phase of anti-Jewish policy, Hitler was thus by no means responding to pressure; he was its decisive instigator.

In initiating the boycott of 1 April, the National Socialist leadership had a wide variety of motives. At this point, National Socialism was in a critical phase of the process of seizing power. The anti-Jewish boycott across the whole country was intended to refocus the activism of Party supporters and at the same time to distract Party activists from other possible targets, such as non-Jewish enterprises or the offices of other parties. The pretext for the boycott was delivered by growing criticism abroad of the violent episodes during the National Socialists' seizure of power. Both this criticism and early moves towards the boycott of German goods abroad were depicted as the machinations of 'international Jewry' for which the German Jews had now to be called to reckoning. The new government thereby made hostages of the German Jews in the very first weeks of its existence.

At the same time, the boycott of Jewish businesses in Germany was intended to set the necessary tone and establish the right atmosphere for the introduction of anti-Semitic legislation. As this propaganda campaign proceeded, public opinion – which was now increasingly controlled by the

National Socialists – was to be given some new material on which to focus: the blame for the numerous difficulties that the new regime was facing was attributed to 'the Jews', against whom defensive action was now legitimate.

The decisive role which Hitler played in the enforcement of the Nazi government's anti-Jewish policy is apparent in the organisation of the boycott of Jewish businesses on 1 April 1933. Although it was Goebbels, Propaganda Chief of the Party and newly appointed Minister of Propaganda, who organised the embargo on Jewish establishments, the decisive initiative was Hitler's. This was confirmed in Goebbels' diary entry for 26 March 1933: according to this account, Hitler called him to to his summer house in Berchtesgaden in the Bavarian Alps in order to inform him of what he called his 'decision':

[we can] only deal with the slanderous attacks from abroad if we lay hold of the originators or at least those who stand to profit from them – namely the Jews who live in Germany and who have so far been left in peace.[3]

Moreover, Hitler took over the full responsibility for calling together a boycott committee consisting of leading NSDAP officials when he made it clear in the Ministerial Conference of 28 March 1933 'that he, the Chancellor of Germany had himself ordered the proclamation issued by the National Socialist Party'.[4] On 6 April 1933, Hitler once again explicitly acknowledged his anti-Semitic policy when, on the occasion of a reception for leading medical officials, he declared that:

it was necessary to satisfy Germany's natural right to its own unique brand of spiritual leadership, and to do this via the

imminent eradication of Jewish intellectuals from the cultural
and spiritual life of Germany.[5]

Later that April Hitler's regime passed three further anti-
Semitic laws: Jews were largely excluded from public office
and from the bar,[6] and a quota for Jewish schoolchildren and
university students was introduced.[7] These laws meant the
end of the equality of Jews in matters of citizenship that had
in principle existed across Germany since 1871.

On the other hand, a series of utterances by Hitler from the
first months of the Third Reich seem to give the impression,
at first sight, that he might have been exercising a rather more
moderate influence on the 'Jewish policy' of the government
and had turned against the more radical elements of the Party.

After Hitler's interventions[8] on the occasion of the anti-
Semitic violence in March 1933, during consultations on the
law on admission to the bar on 7 April he turned against further plans for the exclusion of the Jews and maintained the
view that 'for the moment' they should 'only regulate what is
necessary'. Statutory discrimination against Jewish doctors –
an official proposal to this effect had been submitted to the
cabinet – was 'at the moment not yet necessary'.[9]

On 6 July 1933, in a speech to a conference of the
Reichsstatthalter (Reich Governors, the newly appointed
representatives of the National Socialist government in the
individual German states), Hitler declared:

The front that we must take most notice of today has been set
up outside Germany. This front is dangerous. If we do not
have to deal with it, we must avoid antagonising it. To open
up the Jewish question once more would be to bring the
whole world into turmoil again.[10]

Hitler's attitude of apparent restraint was derived wholly from tactical considerations. Hitler wanted to avoid unnecessary quarrels with his conservative coalition partners; he did not want to put new stress on the already difficult economic situation or to exacerbate the isolation of the Third Reich in matters of foreign affairs.[11]

When he seized power in 1933, Hitler had coherent plans for creating a special legal status for German Jews, over and above any anti-Semitic laws passed. He planned to give them 'alien status' (as he had himself recommended in 1919 and as was enshrined in the NSDAP party manifesto for 1920), and to make their situation gradually worse. His earlier and considerably more far-reaching plans in the area of racial laws and the reasons why these plans had been deferred were clearly elucidated in his speech to the conference of the Reichsstatthalter on 28 September 1933, as the record shows:

As far as the Jewish question is concerned, we cannot draw back from it. The Reich Chancellor said that it would have been preferable to him if we had been able to proceed step-by-step towards an exacerbated treatment of the Jews in Germany – beginning with a citizenship law and from that point on becoming gradually more and more severe with them. However, the boycott [of German goods] instigated by the Jews obliged us to resort immediately to the harshest counter measures. Abroad, he said, they complain mainly about the legal treatment of the Jews as second-class citizens. According to the view most often taken abroad, the most we can do is to refuse citizenship to Jews who present a danger to the State.[12]

4

ATTEMPTING A LEGAL
SOLUTION TO A PROBLEM

The Nuremberg Laws and Anti-Jewish Policy
1935-1937

There was a period of relative calm in the development of National Socialist policy concerning the Jews from the second half of 1933 and throughout 1934,[1] which had come about for reasons connected with foreign and economic policy, and because of relations with the Nazis' coalition partners. Then a second and more radical phase of Jewish persecution began at the beginning of 1935. Party activists once again triggered anti-Semitic violence across the whole country, which they intensified during the spring and summer of 1935. Following their 'established pattern', Party activists once more barricaded Jewish businesses, perpetrated acts of terror against so-called 'racial defilers', prevented marriages between Jews and non-Jews, organised demonstrations and assaulted Jewish citizens. By means of these abuses, the more radical anti-Semitic forces in the Party wanted to push through three core programmatic demands: first, the introduction of a special class of citizenship for Jews; second, prohibitions against marriage as well as sexual relations between Jews and non-Jews; and third, economically discriminatory measures against the Jewish minority.[2]

The violence was part of a campaign on the part of the NSDAP, which wished to shift the internal balance of power in its favour after two years of government. With plans for biological separation and a comprehensive framework of legal discrimination against Jewish minorities, German society was to witness the imposition of radical racist policies that had always been at the heart of National Socialism. The introduction of harsh anti-Jewish measures promised an extension of the National Socialists' power base: the crime of 'racial defilement' (*Rassenschande*) was in future to open the most intimate aspects of a citizen's life to the grossest form of scrutiny; it would in fact remove this kind of intimacy altogether. A citizen's day-to-day life was subjected to the control of informers and spies who were operating in the service of the Party or of the secret police controlled by the National Socialists. The arbitrary deprivation of German citizenship with which the Jews were threatened was an attack on the principles of the rule of law and was designed to undermine the position of the conservative-dominated state apparatus. Which would be the next group to lose the protection of citizenship? And how was one to obtain the *Reichsbürgerrecht* or 'rights of a citizen of the Reich' that had been announced but never more precisely defined? And the plan to exclude Jews from economic life was intended not only to provide immediate economic advantages for the middle-classes, who were so strongly represented in the ranks of the NSDAP; it was aimed at enabling the NSDAP to intervene directly in the economy.

The anti-Jewish campaign was begun at a point when general dissatisfaction amongst the population – in particular with the economic situation – was reaching its height. This growing frustration was also making itself felt amongst the supporters of the NSDAP. By energetically re-activating their 'Jewish policies', the National Socialist leadership was not only attempting to remobilise the Party faithful, it was aiming to recast the whole of public opinion in an anti-Semitic mould. By blaming 'the Jews' for the overwhelming problems that were currently threatening Germany, the Jews would be rigorously severed from the bulk of the general population in all areas of life.

In August 1935, Rudolf Hess, Hitler's 'deputy' in Party matters and Minister of the Interior Frick issued statements in Hitler's name forbidding further 'individual actions'.[3] Once again, Hitler's sole concern was tactical: he wanted to rein in anti-Jewish abuses which were causing unrest and indignation in the population. In essence, however, he shared the same goals as the Party activists.

It was not simply the case that Hitler had made sure that these core anti-Semitic demands were taken up by the NSDAP manifesto in 1920; they had been part of his standard repertoire as a speaker since the beginning of his political career. Since the beginning of the 1920s Hitler had spoken in favour of a ban on 'racial defilement' (a crime that in his eyes even merited the death penalty). He had always declared that permitting Jews to maintain German citizenship was a monstrosity, and he had always wished to exclude the Jews from economic life – in other words, he wished to expropriate Jewish wealth, which he simply declared 'stolen property' belonging to the German people.

It is hardly surprising, then, that Hitler played a decisive role in the late summer of 1935 in the design of the Nuremberg laws, whereby in particular marriage and sexual relations between Jews and non-Jews were forbidden and a special, inferior form of citizenship was defined for Jews. (The Party's third demand, the exclusion of Jews from economic life, was to be postponed for a while).

The decision to include an anti-Jewish law which contained the long-demanded prohibition against 'racial defilement' in the Reichstag session during the Nuremberg Party meeting was made on the evening of 13 September

1935 by a small circle of leading Nazis who had gathered to meet Hitler in a Nuremberg hotel.[4]

The official in charge of the 'Jewish question' (*Judenreferent*) in the Ministry of the Interior, Bernhard Lösener, has given a very vivid account of Hitler's part in creating the anti-Jewish legislation in a memoir written after the war. He describes how he was unexpectedly called to Nuremberg late in the evening of 13 September in order to help with the formulation of a new law.[5] On the next day, according to Lösener's account, together with a group of officials from the ministry, he designed numerous drafts for the law which was later called the 'Law for the Protection of German Blood' (*Blutschutzgesetz*). Minister of the Interior, Wilhelm Frick, presented these drafts to Hitler and then brought them back with specific proposals for amendment. On Saturday 14 September, around midnight, Hitler demanded that four alternative drafts be submitted by the following morning. Furthermore, Lösener goes on to say, Hitler now asked the officials to prepare another law, namely a blueprint of a basic law, a citizenship law for the next day. On the following day Hitler decided on one of the drafts for the 'Law for the Protection of German Blood', and had it passed in the Reichstag, together with the Reich citizenship law that had also been drafted overnight.

After these laws were passed, Hitler declared at the Nuremberg Party Conference that the 'Law for the Protection of German Blood' was 'the attempt to solve by legal means a problem, which, if these means failed repeatedly, would have to be transferred by law to the National Socialist Party for its definitive solution'.[6] He thereby made it clear that he was prepared to use street terror by Party activists (which he had earlier condemned in public declarations) as an instrument for enforcing his policies.

For the following years, there is documentary evidence that Hitler personally directed anti-Jewish policy and regularly intervened in anti-Jewish legislation. The measures in question were mainly concerned with excluding the Jewish minority from the economy, which were measures that had been postponed at the Nuremberg Party Conference.

In the summer of 1936, Hitler charged Göring with preparations for the Four-Year Plan, by which the German economy was to be adapted for war. The memorandum which Hitler sent Göring on this subject clearly shows that preparation for war and further radicalisation of anti-Jewish policy were closely associated in Hitler's thinking. Hitler's position in this matter was that a war against a supposed Bolshevik-Jewish menace was unavoidable:

> Since the outbreak of the French Revolution, the world has been moving ever faster towards a new confrontation. The most extreme solution to this conflict is called Bolshevism and its content and goals are the liquidation [*Beseitigung*] and replacement [*Ersetzung*] of the hitherto leading social stratum of mankind by international Jewry.[7]

In the memorandum, Hitler also explained that preparations for the coming war against 'international Jewry' should in part be financed by the expropriation of Jewish property. To this purpose he demanded two new anti-Jewish laws: first, a law 'which makes all Jews answerable for the damages inflicted upon the German economy and the German people by individual specimens of this criminal phenomenon'; second, he called for the death penalty for what he called economic sabotage, meaning the accumulation of currency reserves abroad. This demand – as further developments would show – was particularly directed against Jewish 'economic sabotage'. It was satisfied by the 'Law to Combat Economic Sabotage', passed in December 1936, which did indeed call for lengthy prison terms or the death penalty for the illegal transfer of property abroad; in the following period it was primarily applied against Jews.[8]

In order to push through the other law that Hitler had proposed in his memorandum on the Four-Year Plan – making the whole of German Jewry comprehensively accountable – a draft of a 'Law Concerning Compensation for Damages inflicted by Jews on the German Reich' was prepared at the beginning of February 1937. After this draft was rejected, because of the anticipated negative implications for the economy, in April 1938 Hitler once more had the Finance Ministry draw up suggestions for a special tax for Jews, which could be raised 'when appropriate (for behaviour by individual Jews that is detrimental to the Volk)'.[9] However, a proposal of this kind drafted by officials in the ministry was not put into practice because it was once again postponed by Göring.[10] It was only after the November pogrom that the project of levying an atonement payment of billions of marks on German Jews was realised.[11]

However, on the other hand, in the spring or early summer of 1937, Hitler decided for a while not to follow up on two important anti-Semitic legislative projects. One was the third decree of the 'Citizenship Law' (*Reichsbürgergesetz*), which was to provide, among other things, for a special trades symbol for non-Jewish businesses. As Frick told Göring in February 1937, this decree was to be promulgated on Hitler's specific orders. Nevertheless in June, on Hitler's instructions once more, the decree was not discussed any further, since the incorporation of holdings owned by foreign Jews would create complications; it was only enacted one year later.[12] Another plan set aside on Hitler's specific orders, in May, was the project to legislate for a special citizenship document.[13]

Hitler continued to be intensely preoccupied with anti-Jewish policy in the years 1936–37 and for tactical reasons was again prepared to be flexible in pressing forward his goals, as is apparent from the different treatment accorded to the various laws, in particular, during this period, to measures for further economic discrimination against Jews.

Hitler's reluctance to radicalise the 'Jewish Question' in the years 1936–37 can be attributed to considerations of foreign and economic policy. The Third Reich had succeeded in gaining a modicum of respectability in its foreign policy. This was manifested in particular in the German-British Naval Agreement in 1935, and in the fact that the victorious powers of the First World War tolerated Germany's transgressions of the Versailles Treaty, both the introduction of general military service in 1935, and the remilitarisation of the Rhineland in 1936. It found expression, above all, in the degree of international participation in the Olympic Games of 1936, and their positive reception.

Economically, Hitler and the National Socialist leadership had by no means abandoned their plan for expropriating Jewish property, but it was highly debatable whether drastic special measures were the best means of achieving this in the economic circumstances prevailing in 1936 and 1937. The exclusion of the Jews from the economy could be achieved much more effectively merely by continuing the gradual process of covertly plundering Jewish wealth (via special taxation measures, confiscation of wealth in the course of currency checks and so on), and by forcing Jewish entrepreneurs whose firms had already been fundamentally weakened

by widespread discrimination and a significant loss of cus-
tomers to sell up – at prices, of course, that fully took into
account any such decrease in value.

So whilst from the outside activity in the field of 'Jewish
policy' appeared to be relatively quiet during the years
1936 and 1937, the regime was merely waiting for the next
opportunity to intensify its persecution of the Jews – an intensification in which the dictator himself showed great personal
interest.

5

THE JEWS MUST BE EXPELLED FROM GERMANY, FROM THE WHOLE OF EUROPE

Pogrom and Total Deprivation of Rights
(1938–1939)

After the end of 1937, concurrent with the National Socialist regime's transition to an expansionist foreign policy, a new and more radical phase in the persecution of the Jews began. Priority was given to the goal of expelling the Jews from Germany; this was principally to be accomplished by means of further discrimination, the direct use of violence and increased economic pressure.

With the transition to an overtly expansionist policy, preparations for which had largely taken the form of reassigning personnel in government and at senior levels of the armed forces, the foreign policy considerations that had hitherto hampered an escalation in the persecution of Jews no longer applied. In addition, Germany's economic position had been consolidated sufficiently for the National Socialists to believe that expropriating the wealth of the remaining, mostly 'aryanised' Jews could be achieved without exposing the overall economy to any significant danger. There was a third reason why persecution was escalated at this point, in this case with a bearing on the internal political situation: the anxieties raised in the population in 1938 by the regime's high-risk foreign policy were once more to be deliberately channelled in the direction of the enemy-figures that had been created by the regime itself, aiming at the ultimate 'removal of the Jews' (*Entjudung*) from German society.

This more radical course was launched by the strongly anti-Semitic address given by Hitler at the Reich Party

Congress in 1937.[1] Amongst other things, in this speech Hitler attacked what in his characteristic anti-Semitic vocabulary he termed 'Jewish-Bolshevist subversion' (*jüdisch-bolschewistische Zersetzung*); the originator of the 'disease' (*Krankheit*) that was Bolshevism was 'that international parasite on nations, which has for many centuries spread across the world, only to reach its full destructive magnitude in our time'.

On 30 November 1937 Joseph Goebbels recorded the following in his diary about a conversation with Hitler which had taken place the previous day:

> Talked about the Jewish question for a long time. […] The Jews must be expelled from Germany, from the whole of Europe. That will take some time still, but it will happen and must happen. The Führer is firmly committed to this.

At the beginning of 1938 the Office for Foreign Affairs of the NSDAP informed the German Foreign Office that, in a conversation with Alfred Rosenberg, Hitler had clearly declared himself in favour of supporting 'Jewish emigration from Germany with all the means at [his] disposal', and that the flood of emigrés would be directed principally towards Palestine.[2]

The territorial expansion of the regime and the radicalisation of the persecution of the Jews were two mutually reinforcing factors. After the Anschluss with Austria in March 1938, National Socialists there, above all in Vienna, bombarded the Austrian Jews with a wave of violence and public humiliation that completely overshadowed the similarly minded activists in the old German territories. However, the consequence of the mass expulsions of the Austrian Jews that resulted from these acts of violence was that the countries who were potentially to receive them began to regulate the influx of Jews from territories under German control and thereby reduced the chances of completely 'removing' the Jews from Germany as a whole. In addition, the long-standing economic pressures on the German Jews meant that they were now increasingly not in a position to make the necessary steps towards emigration.[3]

The overwhelming impression created by the events in Austria motivated the National Socialists in Germany to enforce the expulsion of the Jews not only by introducing new discriminatory legislation – in the first months of 1938 in particular there was a veritable flood of such new measures – but also by intensifying their use of direct acts of violence.[4] As early as 1938, as part of measures to accelerate the expulsion of the Jews from Germany, an action to arrest Jews with a criminal record (even an insignificant one) was initiated across the whole country. Hitler frequently intervened directly in this action. He personally gave the order to include Jews in a general action against 'asocial elements' (*Asoziale*), as is apparent from a note made by the Director of the Jewish Department of the SD (the Security Service of the Nazi Party) on 8 June 1938:

> In a discussion on 1 June 1938 with C [identified by the author as Heydrich], I was confidentially informed that on the orders of the Führer asocial and criminal Jews across the Reich were to be arrested and deployed for the purpose of important earth-moving work.[5]

Hitler was also directly concerned with the propaganda side of the mass arrests. In the course of the ongoing campaign against 'asocial elements' and Jews, and, in order to stir up anti-Semitic feelings, Goebbels asserted in a speech that more than 3,000 Jews had moved to Berlin in the last few months. When Heydrich complained to the Ministry of Propaganda that this was false information, he learned that Goebbels had used the falsified figures 'with the permission of the Führer'.[6] But the arrests in the German capital degenerated into anti-Jewish violence by Party activists egged on by Goebbels, and when this threatened public order and led to critical reports in the foreign press, the violence was stopped on 22 June 'on the Führer's orders', as is clear from a draft report by the Jewish Department of the SD.[7]

Despite the abandonment of the action in Berlin, in a talk with Hitler on 24 July 1938, Goebbels once again confirmed he had the Führer's agreement in principle for a further radicalisation of the persecution.

> We discuss the Jewish question. The Führer approves my measures in Berlin. What the foreign press writes is insignificant. The main thing is that the Jews must be squeezed out. In 10 years they must be removed from Germany. But in the interim we still want to keep the rich ones here as a bargaining counter.[8]

The last sentence already points to the fact that Hitler, in view of increased international tensions, was beginning to think of using the German Jews as hostages.

In the months that followed, the regime steered clear of further anti-Semitic violence, mostly probably because of international tensions during the crisis over the Sudetenland. Immediately after signing the Munich Agreement, at the beginning of October 1938, the anti-Jewish violence was resumed in various areas of Germany as if in response to an order. Before the end of October at least a dozen synagogues were destroyed, the windows of Jewish shops were smashed, Jews were molested, assaulted and in some places even driven from their homes. The pogrom of November 1938 was thus by no means a response by the regime to the attack on the German diplomat Ernst vom Rath by Herschel Grynszpan at the beginning of November in Paris; it was the release of a mood of violent anti-Jewish resentment that had been building up for weeks, if not months.[9]

The course of the November pogrom of 1938 also clearly demonstrates Hitler's personal initiative. It is highly improbable that the news of the death of vom Rath (the event that the Nazis used as an excuse for launching the pogrom) took Hitler by surprise during the Party function in Munich to commemorate the events of 9 November 1923. Rath died in the late afternoon (5.30 p.m. German time); Hitler had expressly sent his personal physician to Paris 'to consult and send a direct report', according to the *Völkischer Beobachter*.[10] Hitler must therefore have been told the news at first hand in the afternoon, and therefore before the Party function had begun, like Goebbels,[11] Nazi Party district leader (Gauleiter) Rudolf Jordan[12] and the Foreign Office, who had been informed independently.[13]

Before Goebbels made his speech on the evening of 9 November, the speech in which he incited the assembled Party leadership to the pogrom, he had already received clear instructions from Hitler, as he noted in his diary:

> Large demonstrations against the Jews in Kassel and Dessau, synagogues set on fire and shops destroyed. In the afternoon the death of the German diplomat vom Rath is announced. Things are ready now. I am going to the party reception in

the old City Hall. Huge crowd. I explain the matter to the
Führer. He decides: allow the demonstrations to continue,
withdraw the police. For once, the Jews shall come to feel the
anger of the people. That is correct.[14]

After giving this instruction to his propaganda minister, Hitler
left the Old Town Hall in Munich and shortly afterwards
Goebbels made his provocative speech. In this speech, which
was an unconcealed incitement to 'hit out' against the German
Jews, Goebbels referred specifically to the instruction Hitler
had just given him, as is evident from the November 1939
report of the Highest Party Court of the NSDAP on the
events that took place on 9 and 10 November 1938:

> On the evening of 9 November 1938 the Minister of
> Propaganda Dr Goebbels[15] informed the leaders of the party
> who had assembled for an evening of comradely entertain-
> ment in the Old Town Hall in Munich that anti-Jewish
> rallies had taken place in the districts of Kurhessen and
> Magdeburg-Anhalt. Jewish businesses had been destroyed and
> synagogues had been set on fire. After hearing Dr Goebbels'
> report, the Führer had decided that whilst the party was not
> responsible for preparing or organising such demonstrations,
> it would not resist them where they arose spontaneously.[16]

Eyewitness reports,[17] according to which Hitler seemed sur-
prised and annoyed about the pogrom in the late evening, if
they are credible at all, can be accounted for by the extent
of the damage in Munich and elsewhere, not however by
the fact that the Party had organised an nationwide
anti-Jewish action for that night. The concept of an 'unsus-
pecting' Hitler is misleading if only because already on

7 November, the day of vom Rath's assassination, Party
activists had provoked violent anti-Jewish excesses in different parts of Germany which were heralded by the Nazi
press as a spontaneous reaction showing the 'anger of the
German population'.[18]

The most important evidence against the thesis that Hitler
had only been informed about the pogrom late in the
evening, and had then immediately stepped in to stop it, is
the report of the Highest Party Court to the effect that the
most important instigator of the pogrom, Goebbels, was
wholly unconcerned at two in the morning when the first
reports of the vandalism and destruction were coming in, and
welcomed it unreservedly later on that morning.[19] Goebbels'
diary entry about his meeting with Hitler at midday on
10 November also shows that Hitler was behind the whole
action: Goebbels was only able to bring the whole campaign
to a stop when Hitler had *approved* the decree on the subject
that he was to issue – a further clear indication that Hitler
bore overall responsibility for the action.[20]

Another document shows that Hitler was far from wishing
to put an end to the pogrom on the night of 9-10 November.
When the office of the Führer's Deputy informed the Party
about instructions from the 'highest possible' level shortly
before three in the morning, they did not demand that the
action be halted but merely that it be channelled in the proper
direction: 'On explicit instructions from the highest possible
level there is to be no setting fire to any Jewish shops or the
like in any case or under any circumstances whatsoever.'[21] This
was in accordance with the tenor of the instructions that had
been issued by the Head of the Gestapo, Heinrich Müller, and
the Director of the Security Police, Heydrich, shortly before
midnight and at 1.20 a.m. respectively.[22]

According to official statistics, the pogrom resulted in ninety-one deaths, but the real total will have been considerably higher, especially if the numerous suicides are included, and those who died during the weeks and months that followed in the concentration camps. Between 25,000 and 30,000 Jewish men were arrested during the pogrom and sent to Buchenwald, Dachau and other camps. Damage to buildings and property was also considerable: more than 100 synagogues were burned down, again according to official statistics, and 7,500 shops and businesses were destroyed.[23] All these violent actions were subsequently approved by the regime as an understandable manifestation of 'spontaneous popular fury'.

After the pogrom, Göring was entrusted by Hitler with the direction and control of further 'anti-Jewish policies'. But whilst Hitler conferred upon Göring the task of scrutinising all decrees relating to the 'Jewish question' before publication,[24] in the months immediately following the pogrom he decided the details of further 'anti-Jewish policies' himself.

After the regime had issued a number of decrees concerning the expropriation of Jewish property on 12 November, Göring disclosed a series of decisions by Hitler in a meeting with leading representatives of Germany and the Party on 6 December.[25] According to these resolutions, there was to be no particular labelling of the Jews, no prohibition against selling to Jews, and a boycott against Jews (*Judenbann*) could be ordered for certain localities.

On 28 December 1938, after a discussion with Hitler, Göring communicated to central Party and state officials the 'authoritative expression of the will of the Führer' concerning further measures to be taken against Jews.[26] In practice this meant that the law for the protection of tenants was not, in general, to be abrogated for Jews, although in 'individual cases steps were to be taken to quarter Jews together in separate houses as far as tenancy agreements permitted'. Jews were not to be permitted to use sleeping and dining cars. The use of 'certain public amenities', such as bath houses or health spas, could be prohibited to Jews. Jews who were civil servants were not to be denied their pensions, but investigations were to be undertaken to see whether or not Jews could manage with lower retirement provision. Jewish welfare organisations were to be allowed to continue to exist. Jewish patents were to be 'aryanised'. In addition, Hitler gave specific orders concerning living accommodation for people in 'mixed marriages' as well as for the 'aryanisation' of their property.

This catalogue is an excellent example of how precisely Hitler's detailed instructions were transmitted by Göring and translated into reality by the bureaucracy.

Thus the Reich Transport Minister forbade Jews the use of sleeping and dining cars on 23 February, in accordance with Hitler's 'stated will'.[27] By means of the law on giving tenancy to Jews of 30 April 1939, the tenancy protection for Jews was substantially curtailed, thereby creating a legal situation that corresponded to Hitler's views on the accommodation of Jews together in separate houses.[28] This law, once again in accordance with Hitler's 'stated will', did however order that German-Jewish mixed families with children be allowed to remain in their homes. With the memo put out by the Minister of the Interior on 16 June 1939 Hitler's wish to restrict the access of Jews to baths and health establishments was fulfilled.[29]

As early as 12 November 1938, at the meeting of leading representatives of the Party and State, which was held under Göring's chairmanship and dealt with further measures of anti-Jewish policy, Göring announced that Hitler would:

now finally undertake a foreign policy initiative, beginning with the powers who had raised the Jewish question, in order to arrive at a proper solution to the Madagascar question. This he explained to me on 9 November. There is now no alternative. He also wants to tell the other states: 'Why are you constantly going on about the Jews? Have them!'[30]

This foreign policy initiative took concrete shape in the following weeks. Hitler entrusted the necessary steps towards it to the President of the Reichsbank, Hjalmar Schacht, who developed a plan originally made by Hans Fischböck, who had been appointed Finance Minister in Austria after the annexation. According to this plan, the emigration of the German Jews was to be financed by an international loan that would facilitate the emigration of approximately 400,000 emigrés able to work and their dependants over a period of between three and five years.[31] Only after Hitler had expressly agreed to this plan,[32] was Schacht able to begin with appropriate enquiries in London at the end of December 1938 and then start concrete negotiations. However, they did not lead to tangible results.[33]

With this foreign policy initiative, the National Socialist regime tried to turn the German 'Jewish problem' into an international question. Memories of the pogrom of 9 November and additional threats were intended both to place pressure upon German Jews to hasten to leave the country and to encourage the international community to prepare to admit a greater number of Jews.

Göring had already stated at the meeting of 12 November that in the event of an international conflict 'an important reckoning with the Jews' would be 'a foregone conclusion',[34] and Hitler expressed himself in similar terms in the course of the following weeks and months. Oswald Pirow, the South African Defence and Finance Minister, who amongst other things was offering Hitler his services as an intermediary in finding an international solution to the German 'Jewish question', was told by his host on 24 November 1938, 'that the problem would be solved in the near future. This was his unshakeable will. But it was not merely a German problem, it was a European problem'.[35] During this conversation, Hitler went as far as making an open threat: 'What do you think Mr Pirow? What would happen in Germany if I lifted my protective hand away from the Jews? The world can not conceive of what would happen.' With this remark, Hitler made it clear to his guest that authority over German anti-Jewish policy ultimately remained with him and that he was in a position to give the signal for a new pogrom at any time – to lift his 'protective hand', as he euphemistically put it. In fact, it was never Hitler's aim to protect the Jews. By presenting himself as a 'protector' of the Jews, he wanted to deflect attention from his own central role in anti-Jewish policy, and he intended to portray any further anti-Jewish violence as a spontaneous outburst of popular fury. Here he was following the official version of events disseminated by the National Socialists after the pogrom of November 1938.

The report on Hitler's official reception for the Czech Foreign Minister, Frantisek Chvalkovsky, on 21 January 1939 contains the following remarks by the Führer: 'The Jews will be exterminated here. The Jews will not get away with what happened on 9 November 1918. This day will be avenged'.[36]

In his speech before the Reichstag on 30 January 1939, the sixth anniversary of the seizure of power,[37] Hitler finally spoke his mind on the 'Jewish question' in a long and pivotal passage:

In my life I have often been a prophet and have usually been ridiculed for it. During my struggle for power it was mostly the Jewish people who laughed at my prophecies that I would some day assume the leadership of the state and thereby of the entire Volk and then, among many other things, bring the Jewish problem to a solution. I believe that the laughter of the Jews in Germany, once so loud, is now sticking in their throats.

Today I will be a prophet once more. If the Jews of international banking within Europe and further afield should succeed once more in plunging the nations into a world war, then the consequence will be not the Bolshevisation of the world and therewith a victory of Jewry; on the contrary, it will be the annihilation of the Jewish race in Europe.

This threat by Hitler had a new quality in that it no longer was aimed only at putting further pressure on the Jews for emigration. Instead, Hitler was now beginning to adjust to the fact that in the case of a world war, a Jewish minority would continue to exist in Germany. He now intended to use this Jewish minority (and any Jews from other countries who might in the case of war fall under his domination) as hostages and thereby prevent an intervention by the Western powers against his war policy. This is why his menaces concentrated on a 'world war' and not merely on 'war'. The threatened 'annihilation' (*Vernichtung*) of the Jews here should be understood as a threat, not clearly defined, but certainly violent.

6

ALL MEASURES AGAINST THE JEWS ARE TO BE DISCUSSED DIRECTLY WITH THE FÜHRER

Hitler's Role in the Persecution of the German Jews, 1933-1939 – An Intermediate Assessment

I t is clear from the chapters so far that, in accordance with his programmatic statements in the 1920s, Hitler systematically pursued a policy of 'removing' the Jews from Germany in the years between 1933 and 1939. To begin with, he did so via a policy of systematic segregation and discrimination, and finally via the direct use of violence. Hitler's direct influence can be demonstrated for all phases of the persecution of the Jews, although the dictator always remained flexible: whilst in general he attempted to radicalise anti-Jewish policies, he was also able to check the radical course of the persecution of the Jews in certain phases, if and when, for internal or foreign policy reasons, this appeared opportune.

It has also become evident that the persecution of the Jews played a central role in Hitler's politics and that the dictator used anti-Jewish policy to try to gain advantages for his regime both within Germany and internationally. With the help of the boycott of Jewish businesses of 1933, international criticism of the terror of the Nazi regime was to be silenced; with the help of anti-Semitic laws, the hope for an immediate economic advantage that was associated with the anti-Semitic aspirations of the Party grass roots would be satisfied; the rearmament programme could only be put into place after the expropriation of Jewish wealth; and finally, Hitler intended to use the Jews as hostages in order to force the compliance of the Western powers. Hitler's anti-Semitic policies are therefore not merely to be seen as the actions of an ideological fanatic; they also had a fundamental role in his power politics.

The fact that at this time Hitler was playing a central role in all questions related to the persecution of the Jews emerges in characteristic fashion from a note of 6 December 1939 issued from the Office of Hitler's Deputy, Rudolf Hess. At the beginning of December 1939, proposals had been made by the Office of the Führer's Deputy about approaching Heinrich Himmler so as to gain powers for confiscating telephones still in Jewish hands and so as to obtain a general identifying mark for Jews. Martin Bormann, Chief of Staff in that Office, and with experience of working closely with Hitler himself, let it be known 'that the Reichsführer SS will discuss all measures against the Jews directly with the Führer'.[1]

7

GRANTING A MERCIFUL DEATH

The Beginning of the War in 1939 and the
Transition to Mass Murder

Durning the war in Poland and in the months thereafter, German SS and police units shot many tens of thousands of people from the Polish elite, including thousands of Jews. These shootings were a part of the policy of the German leadership of rendering Poland leaderless and destroying it as a nation.[1] This policy of mass murder was fully in accord with Hitler's ideas and orders.

On 12 September 1939, when the head of Military Intelligence, Admiral Wilhelm Canaris, drew the attention of General Wilhelm Keitel (Chief of the High Command of the Wehrmacht) to the existing plans for large-scale executions in Poland, Keitel answered, 'this has already been decided by the Führer'. Hitler had made clear that 'if the Wehrmacht does not wish to have anything to do with this then it must also accept that the SS and the Gestapo will become active alongside it.'[2] On 2 October Hitler stated that it was vital to understand that 'no Polish masters should be permitted to exist; where such Poles do exist, they must be killed, harsh though this may sound'.[3]

At the end of May 1940 at a meeting of leading representatives of the police, Hans Frank, the Head of the German occupation administration in Poland (Generalgouverneur) explained the plan for the so-called 'extraordinary pacification' (*Ausserordentliches Befriedungsprogramm*) of Poland, a further chapter in the murder of Polish citizens which was to be completed while the world was distracted by the war in the West. Frank said:

I openly admit that the planned pacification programme will cost the lives of thousands of Poles, especially of those from Poland's intellectual elite. [...] The Führer told me that the treatment and anchoring of German policy in the General-gouvernement [the German occupation administration in Poland] is the business of the relevant persons in the Generalgouvernement alone. He expressed himself thus: 'The leadership elements we have now identified in Poland are what is to be liquidated.'[4]

Alongside the mass murder of the Polish elite groups, in summer and autumn 1939 Hitler ordered a further programme of systematic mass murder, the so-called 'euthanasia' pro-gramme, the systematic killing of patients in institutions.

The 'freedom to destroy lives not fit for living'[5] was a demand that had been made by radical 'racial hygienists' since the 1920s. Hitler made it his own. At the NSDAP Party Congress of 1929 he spoke of what an 'enhancement of strength' it would be if 'Germany could gain a million children every year and remove 700,000 to 800,000 of its weakest inhabitants'; in 1935 he is said to have told the German doctors' leader, Gerhard Wagner, that in the case of war there would be a programme of 'euthanasia'.[6]

In the early phases of the 'euthanasia', there were three inde-pendent programmes. First, in the annexed Polish districts, but also in Pomerania (within the 'old Reich'– Germany's terri-torial border in 1937), SS and police units shot dead thousands of institution patients from autumn 1939 onwards. After November 1939 the sick and disabled who were in hospital were murdered using gas. The SS had built a special gas cham-ber for this purpose in the fortress at Posen. From 1940 onwards, a mobile gas chamber mounted on a lorry was employed for the same purpose.[7] The second phase, the so-called 'children's euthanasia', began on 25 July 1939 when Hitler's personal physician had a heavily deformed child killed in a Leipzig hospital on the instructions of Hitler himself after the child's parents had sought the Führer's permission to take this step. At the same time he sanctioned this individual case, we may suppose that Hitler authorised Karl Brandt and Philipp Bouhler, the Head of the Führer's Chancellery, to do the same thing in similar cases. A procedure for reporting disabled small children was developed and the victims that were identified in this manner were sent to 'specialist children's departments' where they were killed. These murders took place in large numbers at the beginning of the war and probably claimed 5,000 victims in total.[8] The third, at about the same time as the early planning stages of the 'children's euthanasia', possibly in June or July 1939, began when Hitler gave the order for the so-called 'adult euthanasia' in the presence of Heinrich Lammers, Martin Bormann and Leonardo Conti, the Secretary of State in the Interior Ministry.[9] In a relatively short time Brandt and Bouhler succeeded in taking over this task. At a meeting held at the beginning of October the doctors charged with carrying out the euthanasia decided to kill approximately 20 per cent of all patients in special homes and institutions, about 70,000 people in all. One of the most important criteria for the selection of victims was their incapacity to work. The total number of victims originally decided upon was reached by August 1941 in the context of the action entitled 'T4', and the victims were mostly killed in special institutions with the aid of gas.

Since according to the letter of the law those involved in 'euthanasia' were in fact guilty of organising mass murder, and in order therefore to protect them, in October 1939 Hitler gave Bouhler and Brandt a written document of authorisation, and significantly this was dated 1 September 1939, the first day of the war. In this document, which was written on his own letter paper, Hitler gave them the task of granting 'a merciful death' to those who were, 'as far as mankind can judge, terminally ill'.[10]

In the case of 'euthanasia', therefore, Hitler's authorship of and responsibility for the programme is fully demonstrable. This fact is then reinforced, since the programme came to an end or was broken off in August 1941 on Hitler's explicit instructions.

'Euthanasia', or the programme of systematically murdering the inhabitants of institutions, displays remarkable parallels to the systematic murder of the European Jews from 1941/42 onwards. It is possible to see in the 'euthanasia' programme a trial run, in the course of which the regime was collecting significant experience for the *Endlösung* or 'final solution' that was to come. It was not only that, from 1939 onwards, a large number of people were murdered in mass executions and with the aid of gas in special killing centres. It was that a complex procedure had been developed, based on the principle of the division of labour, following which the victims were deceived until the last moment, the perpetrators were apparently relieved of responsibility and the whole programme was to be kept strictly secret. The frequent 'transfer' of the victims, the use of doctors to conduct 'examinations' or selection processes and the introduction of the criterion of 'unfitness for work' are all elements which show clearly the direct links between both programmes of murder. The links between the two programmes are also evident from an organisational perspective: the 'Lange Special Unit', which had been murdering institution patients in the

Warthegau, the province set up from annexed Polish territories, using mobile gas chambers until the summer of 1941, was to be deployed in Chelmno from December of that year for the murder of large numbers of Jews in the same manner. After the end of the 'euthanasia' programme, the personnel carrying out the 'T4' action were to be deployed in building and running the extermination camps in the Polish lands now governed by the German occupation administration (Generalgouvernement Poland). There is one further factor linking both programmes of murder: within the context of 'euthanasia', 4,000–5,000 Jewish patients were murdered, without any exceptions having been made with regard to the nature of the condition or their capacity for work – in contrast to all the other patients.

The authorship of and responsibility for the 'euthanasia' programme, and its close connection with the systematic murder of the Jews are a further significant indicator of Hitler's responsibility for this incomparable crime.

The fact that Hitler left no unambiguous written order in the case of the murder of the European Jews can be attributed to the lessons he learned from the murder of the sick and disabled. It very quickly became clear that an operation of such magnitude simply could not be kept secret. On the contrary, these murders became known to the population and provoked expressions of disquiet and protests; formal reports were even lodged with the courts. This resistance will have been a significant reason for breaking off the 'euthanasia' programme. If it had become known that Hitler had given written authority for 'euthanasia', his aura as Führer would have suffered some considerable damage.

When in 1941/42 the systematic murder of the European Jews was set in train, it will have been this experience that prevented Hitler from assuming responsibility for the new programme of murder by making an unambiguous written statement. Furthermore, two years' experience of war and mass murder had also made those responsible for conducting the programme feel secure that they could carry out the murder of the Jews even without being covered formally by the highest authority in the Third Reich.

8

AN ATTEMPT AT THE SETTLEMENT AND REGULATION OF THE JEWISH PROBLEM

Plans for a 'Jewish Reservation' in Poland

The systematic murder of 10,000 people in Poland and the beginning of the 'euthanasia' programme are the background against which the 'Jewish policy' of the Third Reich in the months after the beginning of the war should be considered. Plans were now being made for establishing a 'reservation' (*Reservat*) in Poland for all the Jews under German domination. In this case as well, Hitler's influence on the plans was decisive: in a meeting with his heads of departments, Heydrich, the chief of the Security Police, reported on 14 September 1939 that Hitler was given proposals regarding 'the Jewish problem in Poland by the Reichsführer [identified by the author as Himmler] about which only the Führer could make a decision because they carried significant foreign policy consequences'.[1]

On 21 September Heydrich was able to report to the heads of department of the Security Police that Hitler had in the meantime made a decision on the issue of the deportations. 'The deportation of Jews into the foreign-language Gau, deportation across the demarcation line, has been approved by the Führer.' By 'foreign-language Gau' was meant those occupied areas not directly annexed to Germany which were later to become the Generalgouvernement Poland; 'demarcation line' referred to the line on which the Soviet Union and the German Reich in Poland had agreed in order to divide their spheres of interest. In his report on 21 September Heydrich gave further information about the planned deportations:

However, the whole process is to take place over the course
of one year. The Jewry is to be brought together in the cities
in ghettos in order to keep better control and to make later
deportation easier. The first priority is the disappearance of
the Jew as a small settler in the countryside. This action must
be carried out within the next 3 to 4 weeks.[2]

On 29 September Hitler explained his plans for the newly
conquered Polish territory to Rosenberg, the Head of the
Office for Foreign Affairs of the NSDAP. He said he had
envisaged three strips: the area between the Vistula and the
Bug was where the Jews from the whole of Germany were
to be settled, as well as 'all in any way unreliable elements'; at
the Vistula an 'East Wall' was to be built, and on the former
German-Polish border there was to be a 'broad belt of
Germanification and colonisation'; between them was to be
a sort of Polish 'state authority'.[3] The idea of a 'Jewish reservation' in Poland was addressed relatively frequently in the
coming weeks by Hitler and other prominent National
Socialists. Thus for example, it was expressly mentioned by
Hitler to the Swedish industrialist Birger Dahlerus when he
visited Germany at the end of September in the course of his
mediation attempts for peace between Germany and Great
Britain.[4] On 1 October Hitler spoke to the Italian Foreign
Minister about the idea of a 're-allocation of land on ethnic
lines' (*volkliche Flurbereinigung*) in the East.[5] The German press
was also secretly briefed on these plans.[6] On 6 October Hitler
declared in a speech before the Reichstag that the 'most
important task' which results from the 'collapse of the Polish
state' is a 'new order in ethnographic relations, that is to say a
re-settlement of nationalities'. In the second part of his
speech, Hitler gave notice that in the course of the coming

'ordering of the all the space available for living (*Lebensraum*) according to nationalities' – which was to include all of Europe under German influence – 'an attempt at the settlement and regulation of the Jewish problem will be undertaken'.[7]

Directly after this speech, on 7 October 1939, Hitler signed his edict on the 'consolidation of German ethnicity' (*Festigung deutschen Volkstums*). By doing so Hitler set Himmler two tasks: the first was 'to take in and settle within the Reich [...] German people who have previously been forced to live far away'; the second was to 'organise the settlement of national groupings in such a way as to set up stricter dividing lines between them'. In this edict Hitler not only charged Himmler with returning to Germany German nationals and ethnic Germans (*Reichs- und Volksdeutsche*) coming from abroad and with 'creating new German settlements through deportation'; he specifically entrusted him with the 'exclusion of the damaging influence of those alien portions of the population who imply danger for the Reich and the community of the German people'. In another section of the edict, Hitler specified that 'the population groups in question can be assigned to specific living areas'.[8]

While Himmler started preparations for the deportation of Poles and Jews from the annexed Polish areas in accordance with these orders, Adolf Eichmann concerned himself with preparations to deport Jews from the rest of the Greater German Reich (Germany and territories added to Germany after 1938), also explicitly responding to orders issued by Hitler. Eichmann was at this point Director of the Central Office for Jewish Emigration in Prague, which worked under Gestapo instructions to deport Jews systematically from the 'Protectorate of Bohemia and Moravia' (the occupied Czech

heartland), and on 6 October he received an additional order
from Gestapo chief Heinrich Müller to deport Jews from the
Kattowitz district (i.e the recently annexed Polish area) as
well as from Moravia–Ostrava (in the Protectorate) and to
send them to Nisko am San in the District of Lublin in the
Generalgouvernement Poland. His assignment was soon
extended, on orders from Hitler, to cover the deportation of
all Jews from Germany. Thus he stated to Josef Wagner,
the Gauleiter of Silesia, on 10 October, 'the Führer has for the
present ordered the relocation of 300,000 Jews from
the Altreich [Germany's territorial border in 1937] and the
Ostmark.'[9] While visiting Vienna on 7 October, Eichmann
explained to the Special Commissioner for Jewish questions
in the Office of the Reich Governor for Austria, 'according
to strictly confidential information from the director of the
Central Office for Emigration of Jews, the Führer has given
the order that, to initiate the whole operation, 300,000 less
well-off Jews from the Greater German Reich area [will be
deported] to Poland'. In the meantime, those Jews still living
in Vienna are to be seized and deported within the context
of an operation which will take 'at most half of a year'.[10]

Just as this first extensive deportation programme was covered by Hitler's personal authority, so the cessation of the
Nisko experiment is also traceable to a decision by Hitler. On
17 October, after the first deportation trains had reached
Nisko with altogether about 4,700 people from Vienna,
Moravia–Ostrava and Kattowitz, Hitler told Keitel that
measures must be taken to ensure that the future
Generalgouvernement Poland 'has military importance for us
as an advance glacis and can be used as an area in which to
assemble troops for the attack'. This perspective was obviously not compatible with that of a 'Jewish reservation'; the

deportations to Nisko were stopped on the order of Germany's Security Head Office.[11] Seen from the perspective of the long term, Hitler said, the 'running of this area' must 'make it possible for us to clean the Reich of Jews and Polacks' – a further indication that he had in no way abandoned the basic idea of a 'Jewish reservation' in the General-gouvernement Poland.[12]

9

SOME TIME IN THE FUTURE WE WANT TO SHIP THE JEWS OUT TO MADAGASCAR

Hitler and the Madagascar Plan

After the victory over France in June 1940, the plan to push the Jews into a 'reservation' (*Reservat*) in Poland was replaced with another project for the territorial solution of the Jewish problem, the so-called Madagascar plan.

As early as 25 May Himmler had presented Hitler with a memorandum which included the following key sentence with respect to the fate of the Jews: 'By means of the possibility of a large emigration of all Jews to Africa or to some other colony I hope to see the concept of Jew completely extinguished.' In the same document Himmler had, 'because of an inner conviction', rejected 'the Bolshevist methods for the physical extirpation (*Ausrottung*) of a people as un-German and impossible'. Hitler judged this memorandum to be 'very good and correct', according to Himmler's note of 28 May. However, the document was 'to be kept completely secret', Himmler was to show it to Hans Frank at some point 'in order to tell him that the Führer thinks it is right'.[1]

The manner in which Hitler treated this suggestion is perfectly characteristic of his style of leadership. He gave no direct instructions but left it to Himmler to follow up the matter, giving him explicit authority to refer to his, Hitler's, authority. The documents show that the project got underway during the following months.

Plans for the re-settlement of altogether 4 million Jews on Madagascar, an island off the east coast of Africa, were worked out in the German Department of the Foreign Office,[2] as well as in the German Security Head Office.[3] From the surviving records of the German Foreign Office it is clear that the Madagascar plan (like the plan of a 'Jewish reservation' in Poland) was not a new variation on an emigration solution to the 'Jewish problem', but instead had the function of using the Jews living under German control as hostages; in this way they could be used to prevent the United States from entering the war. Thus in a note from the Jewish expert of the German Department, Rademacher, it is claimed that under a German police governor 'the Jews should be set up as a bargaining-counter under German control to ensure the future good behaviour of their racial associates in America'.[4] In another note, the same expert wrote that the Security Police was 'experienced in the appropriate manner in which to carry out punishment measures that had become necessary because of unfriendly activities by Jews in the USA against Germany'.[5] The mere fact that Madagascar lacked the basic conditions necessary for existence of 4 million European Jews makes it clear that the plan itself was a threat to the continued existence of Jews in the area under German control.

Hitler's great interest in the Madagascar plan is documented sufficiently. Hitler and the Head of the German Foreign Office, Joachim von Ribbentrop, sketched out the plan to their Italian guests, Benito Mussolini and Galleazzo Ciano, during their talks in Munich on 17 and 18 June.[6] Hitler mentioned the Madagascar project on 20 June to the Commander-in-Chief of the Navy, Erich Raeder.[7] On 12 July the leader of the Generalgouvernement Poland, Frank, informed his colleagues of a conversation with Hitler that had taken place four days earlier:

Another very important matter is the decision of the Führer, stemming from a proposal of mine, that there be no further transports of Jews into the Generalgouvernement Poland. In general political terms I would like to say that it is planned to transport the entire Jewish clan from the German Reich, the Generalgouvernement Poland and the Protectorate to an African or American colony in the shortest conceivable time span following the peace settlement. Madagascar is being considered; it would be separated from France for this purpose.[8]

At the beginning of August, in a discussion with Otto Abetz, the Ambassador to Paris,[9] Hitler returned to the plan of the expulsion (*Vertreibung*) of all Jews from Europe, and a similar statement by Hitler made on 16 August is mentioned in Goebbels' diary: 'Some time in the future we want to ship the Jews out to Madagascar. There they too can set up their own state.'[10]

10

ACCORDING TO THE WILL OF THE FÜHRER

Deportation and Plans for Deportation
(1940-1941)

Hitler's great interest in the further development of 'Jewish policy' is manifested particularly by his personal involvement in subsequent plans for deportation over the following months.

The initiative for the deportation to France of approximately 7,000 Jews from the two Gaue (i.e. Party districts), Baden and the Saar-Palatinate area, which took place on 22 and 23 October 1940, most probably lay with the two responsible Gauleiter, Josef Bürckel and Robert Wagner.[1] These transportations were specifically approved by Hitler, as is clear from a handwritten note by the Jewish expert of the foreign office, Franz Rademacher.[2]

Whilst these deportations can readily be interpreted as preparations for the planned expulsion of the European Jews to Madagascar, Hitler's statements in the following months show that he was turning his attention away from Madagascar as a potential destination for deportees and thinking more seriously once more of the Generalgouvernement Poland. The Madagascar plan was eventually dropped at the end of 1940: the length of the war with Great Britain had rendered the African island unreachable.

At the beginning of November 1940, Hitler made a personal decision concerning the distribution of 200,000 ethnic Germans (*Volksdeutsche*) who were to be accommodated in the territories of Germany before the end of the year, thanks to agreements with the Soviet Union and Rumania negotiated in

September and October. In this connection, on the occasion of a conference with leading military personnel on 4 November, he made a decision about the further deportation of Poles and Jews from the annexed Eastern territories to the General-gouvernement Poland: 'Gouvernement: plus 150-160 thousand Poles and Jews from the newly conquered territories'.[3]

On the very same day, discussions began on the agreement to a quota for those to be deported from the areas that had formerly been Poland and had been annexed by Germany, as we learn from Goebbels' diaries. According to this source, Hitler had 'laughed' when he created 'peace' between Gauleiter Erich Koch (from East Prussia) and Gauleiter Albert Forster (Danzig-West Prussia):

> Everyone wants to throw their rubbish in to the General-gouvernement Poland: Jews, the sick, the lazy, etc. And Frank resists. Not entirely without justification. He would like to make a model country out of Poland. That is going too far. He can not and should not do this. Poland should be a large work reservoir for us – this is what the Führer has decided. [...] And the Jews – we will throw them out of these areas later as well.[4]

At this same meeting or directly thereafter, deportation quotas were set for the two Gaue – and according to this commit-ment mass deportations of more than 47,000 Poles (Jews and non-Jews) from the annexed territories into the General-gouvernement Poland followed in the next months.[5]

At the beginning of December, Lammers informed Baldur von Schirach (the Gauleiter of Vienna) that his wish, first expressed two months earlier, for the deportation (*Abschiebung*) of Vienna Jews had been approved by Hitler.

This is further proof of Hitler's direct involvement in the plans for deportation:

> As Reichsleiter Bormann has informed me, the Führer has decided on the basis of one of your reports that 60,000 Jews who are living in the Reichsgau of Vienna should be deported to the Generalgouvernement Poland as rapidly as possible, i.e. while the war is still going on, because of the housing shortage in Vienna.[6]

In anticipation of this deportation, beginning in February/March, 5,000 Jews from Vienna were deported to the Generalgouvernement Poland.[7]

After the Madagascar plan had became obsolete by autumn 1940 because of the continuation of the war in the West, and after a comprehensive deportation of the Jews from German-controlled areas into the Generalgouvernement Poland had for various reasons proved to be difficult, Hitler assigned the responsibility for deporting the Jews to the occupied Soviet areas to the Reich Security Main Office (Heydrich's office where he directed the various branches of the security apparatus including the Gestapo, the Criminal Police, and the SD). This decision, which was made parallel to the preparations for 'Barbarossa' in late 1940 and early 1941, can be reconstructed on the basis of a series of documents.

On 21 January, the Gestapo's Jewish expert in Paris, Theodor Dannecker, noted the following in a paper prepared for Adolf Eichmann:

> According to the will of the Führer, after the war the Jewish question within the German-controlled or German-dominated parts of Europe should be pursued towards a

definitive solution [*endgültige Lösung*]. The chief of the Security Police and the SD [Heydrich] has already received a mandate from the Führer – via the RF-SS [Himmler] or through the Reichsmarschall [Göring] to submit a proposal for a final solution project [*Endlösungsprojekt*]. On the basis of the wide experience of the departments of the CdS [Chief of the Security Police] and SD in the treatment of the Jews, and thanks to the lengthy preparations made in this domain, the most significant features of this project have been worked out. It is now in the hands of the Führer and the Reichsmarschall.

It is clear that the execution of this plan entails an enormous amount of work and that it can only be successful if the greatest care is taken in its preparation. This must be based upon a comprehensive deportation of the Jews as well as upon the planning of a settlement action prepared to the smallest detail to take place in a territory which has not yet been decided upon.[8]

In addition we learn from a statement to the Propaganda Ministry submitted on 20 March 1941 by Eichmann, who had been head of the department in the Reichssicherheitshauptamt responsible for 'evacuation matters' (*Räumungsangelegenheiten*) since December 1939, that

Pg. Heydrich, who had been commissioned by the Führer with the final evacuation of Jews, had presented the Führer with a proposal 8 to 10 weeks earlier which had not been implemented for the sole reason that the General-gouvernement Poland was not at that point in a position to accept a single Jew or Pole from the old Reich.[9]

Taking these various pieces of information together, it becomes clear that, sometime before January 1941, Heydrich had received a commission from Hitler (via Himmler and Göring) to prepare a first draft for a 'final solution project' to be realised 'after the War' for the total deportation of all Jews into a territory yet to be decided. This plan was ready in January 1941, but because of the situation in the General-gouvernement Poland it could not be implemented. On 15 March the deportations to the Generalgouvernement Poland were halted because of the transport situation that had arisen in view of military preparations for the attack on Russia.[10]

Apparently completely unaffected by the halt to deportations which had been called two days earlier, those gathered at Hitler's luncheon table on 17 March conversed about further deportation programmes, as Goebbels described almost euphorically in his diary:

> Vienna will soon be totally free of Jews. And now it is Berlin's turn. I discuss this with the Führer and with Dr Franck [sic]. He sets the Jews to work and they are also obedient. Later they must leave Europe entirely.[11]

Frank, who had in the meantime returned once more to the Generalgouvernement Poland, also expressed himself on the issue of Hitler's further plans concerning the persecution of the Jews. Thus the minutes of a meeting of 25 March read as follows:

> SS–Ogruf [Obergruppenführer, SS-General] Krüger announced the provisional stoppage of the resettlement of Poles and Jews in the Generalgouvernement Poland. Frank

says that the Führer has told him that the Generalgouvernement Poland will be the first area made free of Jews.[12]

From these statements by Frank and Goebbels we thus can
conclude two things: first, that the Generalgouvernement
Poland was not the final destination for the intended 'evacuation of the Jews' because it was itself to be made 'free of
Jews' and the Jews were to 'leave Europe altogether'; second,
that the assurances given by Hitler to Goebbels and Frank to
make their respective areas of domination 'free of Jews' were
promises that could only be realised over the long term. What
Hitler's timetable for a 'Germanisation' of the Generalgouvernement Poland really was can be deduced from
another statement by Frank, made on the same day, 25 March
1941: 'In the course of the next 15 to 20 years, the Führer is
decided to make this area [the Generalgouvernement Poland]
a purely German land.' Shortly thereafter Frank moved on to
planning the Warsaw Ghetto, which implied at least a
medium-term existence for the Jewish inhabitants of
Warsaw.[13] Goebbels' diary entry for 22 March also shows that
the Propaganda Minister had in the meantime understood
that the 'evacuation' from Berlin could only be implemented
over a longer period of time: 'The Jews can not be evacuated
from Berlin since 30,000 work in the armaments industry
there.'

And indeed, by March 1941 at the very latest, the Nazi
leadership was clear about the true destination planned for
the Jews who, long-term, were to be expelled from 'the whole
of Europe': they were to be deported to the newly conquered
Eastern territories after the war against the Soviet Union for
which Hitler had concretely begun preparations as early as
the last months of 1940.[14]

More evidence for this intention is supplied by a memo by Heydrich from 26 March 1941 concerning a discussion with Göring:

> In relation to the solution of the Jewish question, I reported briefly to the Reichsmarschall and showed him my draft, which he accepted, with one alteration regarding Rosenberg's jurisdiction, and which he ordered me to resubmit.[15]

By 'Rosenberg's jurisdiction' was meant the latter's designated role as chief of an authority that was to administer the eastern occupied territories – what was later to become the Ministry for the Occupied Eastern Territories. This makes it clear that the planned 'solution to the Jewish question' was to take place in the soon-to-be-occupied areas of the Soviet Union. The draft was resubmitted on 31 July 1941, when Göring entrusted Heydrich with the responsibility for 'preparations in organisational, technical and material respects for the complete solution to the Jewish question in the German area of influence in Europe',[16] taking into account the 'jurisdictions of other central authorities'.

What those involved in the preparation of 'Barbarossa' actually understood by the term 'final solution' within the Soviet Union after it was conquered is not clear. Before the start of 'Operation Barbarossa', the German attack upon the Soviet Union, no preparations had been made for a 'reservation' or for mass murder. Just as with the plan for a 'reservation' in Poland and with the Madagascar plan, in the case of a deportation to the Soviet Union the European Jews would have met with a situation in which the basic conditions for human existence were not present – particularly since German policy there consisted of the starvation of the Soviet population.[17]

Death on a massive scale would have been the inevitable consequence.

For the months before 'Barbarossa' there is a series of concrete indications that Hitler in particular had declared himself in favour of such a comprehensive deportation 'to the East'. Frank explained to Goebbels directly before the beginning of the attack on the Soviet Union that he was preparing for the banishment (*Abschiebung*) of the Jews, as reported in the Goebbels diaries:

> Dr Franck [sic] talks about the Generalgouvernement Poland. There they are already looking forward to being able to banish the Jews. Jewry in Poland is gradually decaying. A justified punishment for having incited the people and instigated war. The Führer has also prophesied this to the Jews.[18]

From statements which he made a few weeks later, it becomes clear why Frank was so certain: he informed his staff on 17 July 1941 that there would be no further ghetto construction in the Generalgouvernement Poland; according to an assurance that Hitler had given him on 19 June, in the foreseeable future the Jews would be removed from the Generalgouvernement Poland, which would then become a 'transit camp' (*Durchgangslager*).[19]

A further source is a complaint that the Rumanian Head of State, Ion Antonescu, made to Hitler on 16 August 1941. Antonescu complained that Bessarabian Jews who had been expelled from their homes by Rumanian troops and had been forced further to the east, to Ukraine, were now being pushed back from there by the Wehrmacht. This practice, according to Antonescu, was in contravention of 'the guidelines regarding the treatment of Eastern Jews given to him by the Führer in Munich'.[20] According to Antonescu, he had been told during his meeting with Hitler in Munich on 13 June 1941 that the Jews of Eastern Europe were to be deported to the conquered Soviet areas, and this is what his troops did right away, without waiting for the end of the war as Hitler had intended that they should.

This chapter shows, then, that Hitler gave his full approval to the plans of the *Reichssicherheitshauptamt* for the deportation of the Jews to the Soviet Union once it had been conquered.

11

THE JEWISH-BOLSHEVIK INTELLIGENTSIA... MUST BE ELIMINATED

The Conduct of the War and Mass Shootings, Summer 1941

In the course of the preparations for the racist war of extermination against the Soviet Union, it was Hitler who converted Nazi ideological thought into concrete instructions. On 3 March 1941 Hitler gave instructions to Alfred Jodl, the Chief of the Leadership Staff of the Wehrmacht, for a new version of a proposal presented to him by the High Command of the Wehrmacht (OKW) on the 'guidelines for special areas relating to instruction no. 21', which was to constitute the basis for the occupation administration in the Soviet territories that were to be conquered:

> The forthcoming campaign is more than just an armed struggle; it will also lead to the conflict of two world views. In order to end this war, given the vastness of the territory, it will not suffice merely to defeat the enemy army. [...] The Jewish–Bolshevik intelligentsia, hitherto the oppressor of the people, must be eliminated.[1]

A week before this, whilst reporting to Göring, the leader of the OKW Armaments Office, Georg Thomas, had learned of Hitler's view that 'the Bolshevik leaders had first to be dealt with quickly'.[2]

In accordance with Hitler's orders of 3 March, Jodl issued the 'directive concerning the special areas of Barbarossa' on 13 March.[3] In this directive it says:

In the army's operational area, the Reichsführer SS is granted special responsibilities on behalf of the Führer for the preparation of the political administration; these special responsibilities arise from the struggle that has ultimately to be acted out between two opposing political systems. In the context of these responsibilities, the Reichsführer SS will act independently and on his own responsibility.

What the military understood by these 'special responsibilities' becomes clear from Jodl's directive of 3 March for the compilation of the definitive version of the guidelines, in which he had spoken of the 'necessity for rendering all Bolshevik chieftains and commissars harmless without delay'.[4]

The tenor of Hitler's statement of 17 March to the highest ranks in the army was just as explicit:

The intelligentsia installed by Stalin must be destroyed. The leadership machine of the Russian empire must be defeated. In the Greater Russian area the use of the most brutal force is necessary.[5]

On 30 March, Hitler made a similar speech to a meeting of Generals, as Chief of the General Staff of the Army, General Halder, records in abbreviated fashion:

Struggle of two world views against one another. Devastating judgement about Bolshevism — it is akin to asocial criminality. Communism immense danger for the future. We must move away from the standpoint of soldierly camaraderie. The Communist is not a comrade, neither before nor after. We are talking about a war of extermination [*Vernichtung*]. If we do not look at it this way than we might well beat the enemy, but in 30 years we will once again be faced with the Communist enemy. We are not waging war in order to conserve the enemy. [...] War against Russia: extermination of the Bolshevik Commissars and the Communist intelligentsia.[6]

The 'Directive on the Exercise of Jurisdiction and Particular Measures by the Troops' signed by Hitler on 13 May 1941 determined that criminal offences committed by members of the Wehrmacht against the civilian population in the Soviet areas to be conquered were no longer automatically to be punished by Wehrmacht courts, but would be dealt with by these only in special cases. In addition, military courts would no longer be responsible for 'criminal offences committed by enemy civilians' at all; these were to be punished by the troops directly as and when they occurred. The 'Guidelines for the Treatment of Political Commissars' signed by Keitel, the Chief of the OKW, on 6 June also corresponded closely to Hitler's instructions: they made provision for shooting this entire group of people. The 'Guidelines for the Behaviour of the Troops in Russia' issued on 19 May also matched Hitler's conception of the conduct of the war in the East: they encouraged 'drastically ruthless and energetic measures against Bolshevik agitators, guerillas, saboteurs and Jews'.

In accordance with the guidelines of 3 March that had been made more rigorous on Hitler's instruction, the Army High Command (OKH) and the Reichsführer SS were in agreement about deploying 'special units (*Sonderkommandos*) of the Security Police and the SD in the army's operational area' and that these were to carry out 'their tasks on their own responsibility', as contained in the order from the OKH dated 28 April 1941.[7]

In order to put this agreement into practice, Himmler decided on 21 May that Higher SS and Police Leaders should be deployed in the Eastern areas that were to be occupied, and that 'in order to carry out tasks assigned directly by me', SS and police troops and security police were to be subordinate to the Higher SS and Police Leaders or HSSPF (as regional representatives of Himmler who were able to use Himmler's authority to override other branches of the SS and police).[8]

The leaders of the special units received oral instructions from Heydrich shortly before their departure. Their exact formulation is not known, but their substance can be reconstructed on the basis of two written documents by Heydrich.[9] Heydrich's note to the heads of the *Einsatzgruppen* (task forces consisting of SS and police personnel surbordinate to the Reich Security Office or *Reichssicherheitshauptamt*) of 29 June referred to the order previously issued orally to foster 'self-cleansing efforts' (*Selbstreinigungsbestrebungen*), i.e. pogroms of the Jewish population. These 'self-cleansing efforts by anti-Communist or anti-Jewish groups in the area to be occupied' were, according to Heydrich's instructions, 'not to be hindered'. Instead, they were to be 'initiated without betraying the identity of the initiators, to be intensified where necessary, and to be steered in the right direction'.[10]

In a further note dated 2 July, Heydrich informed the Higher SS and Police Leaders of 'instructions of the greatest importance issued by me to the special units and commando groups of Security Police and the SD'.[11] Here it was once more a question of 'self-cleansing efforts (*Selbstreinigungsversuche*) of anti-Communist or anti-Jewish circles in the areas to be occupied' which were 'not to be hindered', but to be encouraged, again 'without leaving a trace'.

Furthermore, in the same note from 2 July, Heydrich listed under the key word 'executions' those groups of persons who were to be shot by the *Einsatzgruppen*:

To be executed are all:
  – functionaries of the Comintern (as well as all professional Communist politicians)
  – the higher, middle and radical lower functionaries of the Party, the Central Committees, the district and regional committees
  – people's commissars
  – Jews in Party and state posts
  – other radical elements (saboteurs, propagandists, snipers, assassins and agitators, etc.)

This order is certainly not to be interpreted as meaning that Heydrich intended to limit executions to those Jews who held 'Party and state posts'. Given the fact that in the course of war preparations the supposedly close connection between Jews and the Soviet system was repeatedly emphasised, it can be concluded that the instructions to execute 'other radical elements' were primarily directed against the Jewish population. Even the last word of this list, 'etc.', shows that the circle of 'other radical elements' was by no means clearly delineated.

The idea that efforts were made from the beginning to limit the set of Jewish victims specifically to 'all [...] Jews in Party and State posts' is also incompatible with the intention of allowing collaborators to initiate these 'self-cleansing operations', or pogroms and massacres. A pogrom once begun could not be confined to specific Jewish victims chosen according to their function.

The massacres by the four *Einsatzgruppen* (the task forces consisting of SS and police personnel subordinate to the Reich Security Office) commenced with the beginning of the war in the East. They are extensively documented, above all in the situational reports (*Ereignismeldungen*) for the USSR, put out by the Reich Security Office; these reports openly describe the murder of hundreds of thousands of people, more than 90 per cent of them Jews.[12]

From the reports and other sources it is evident that at first, in accordance with their orders, the *Einsatzgruppen* supported pogroms initiated by the local population and began at the same time to carry out mass executions of Jewish men.[13] The way in which the units acted was not completely uniform, and much depended on the initiative of each of the unit commanders and on local circumstances. However, a closer investigation of the events demonstrates that a unified model for the activities of the units can in fact be reconstructed.

Thus pogroms were initiated mainly by *Einsatzgruppen* A and B during their advance through the Baltic States[14] in particular in Kovno,[15] Vilna,[16] Riga[17] and in other Latvian and Lithuanian cities.[18] The experience of these *Einsatzgruppen* was that the pogroms could be sparked off partly by 'appropriate influence' on the auxiliary police who were made up of local men.[19]

Pogroms initiated by the Germans can be shown to have been the work of *Einsatzgruppe* C in various cities and localities in Western Ukraine, in the former Polish districts that had been under Soviet occupation since 1939, particularly in Lvov[20] and Tarnopol.[21] In many cases it is not possible to reconstruct whether the initiative for the more than fifty pogroms that can be proved in these areas in summer 1941 stemmed from the German side or from Ukrainian nationalists. Proper analysis here is made even more difficult because the Organisation of Ukrainian Nationalists (OUN) was to a significant extent steered by the Germans.[22]

However, at the end of July *Einsatzgruppe* C was forced to admit[23] the local population was no longer prepared to incite pogroms.[24] *Einsatzgruppe* A had also come to the conclusion in July that pogroms could only be brought about in the first days after occupation.[25]

Mass executions of Jewish men can be proved for almost all *Einsatzgruppen* from the first weeks of the war onwards. This is true of three of the four units in *Einsatzgruppe* A,[26] and also of its subordinate group, the 'Tilsit special unit' (*Sonderkommando* Tilsit), which carried out large-scale massacres in the border area immediately after the war had begun. This is also true of all four units of *Einsatzgruppe* B,[28] for all four units of *Einsatzgruppe* C[29] and for *Einsatzgruppe* z.b.V., which was recruited from amongst the Security Police of the Generalgouvernement Poland and had been sent to support *Einsatzgruppe* C in the Eastern Polish regions.[30] Mass executions of Jewish men can also be proved for all five units of *Einsatzgruppe* D up to the beginning of August 1941,[31] and also for various battalions of the German police.[32]

The various special units and police units quickly began shooting not only particularly 'suspicious' people or 'Jews in Party and State posts', but all persons who belonged to a very vaguely defined Jewish 'intelligentsia' or elite. In the first weeks of the war, many units also shot Jewish men of military age and in some places all men in this age group.

The units were instructed to carry out this radical procedure by Himmler, Heydrich and other high-up SS commanders, who undertook frequent tours of inspection amongst their units during these critical weeks and months.

The unit commanders thus obviously had a certain room for manoeuvre in which they were first left to their own initiative; when they did not live up to expectations, the higher level of command gave them guidance.

Himmler and Heydrich accordingly appeared in the German-Lithuanian border area at the end of June, where they were briefed on the mass shootings of the Tilsit special unit, which they then approved 'in their entirety'.[33] Shortly afterwards Heydrich gave the 'commanders of the SPSD [Security Police and Security Service – the Nazi Party intelligence service] and the units of the State Police in the East permission' – after the model of the Tilsit special unit – 'to carry out cleansing operations in the newly occupied areas opposite their own sectors of the border for the purpose of relieving the *Einsatzgruppen* and *Einsatzkommandos*, and above all in order to secure for them the greatest possible freedom of movement'.[34]

On 30 June Himmler and Heyrich came to Grodno in Lithuania and complained that the sections of unit EK 9 deployed there and in Lida had so far liquidated 'only 96 Jews'. The commander of *Einsatzgruppe* B at once gave the order 'to intensify activity here significantly'.[35] On 9 July Himmler and Heydrich appeared in Grodno again[36] and were able to satisfy themselves that the command of *Einsatzgruppe* B to extend the range of liquidations had by then been followed.

According to the testimony of Higher SS and Police Leader, Erich von dem Bach-Zelewski, during a discussion with officers of the SS and the Police in Bialystok, Himmler said, 'all Jews are to be regarded as partisans, without exception'.[37] On the following day, Daluege, Chief of the uniformed civilian police force (*Ordnungspolizei*) who had also appeared in Bialystok announced to members of the

Police Regiment Mitte that 'Bolshevism would now finally be exterminated'.[38] Two days later, on 11 July, the commander of the Police Regiment Mitte in Bialystok ordered the shooting of all Jewish men between the ages of seventeen and forty-five who have been arrested for plunder.[39] The police made the 'conviction' of the Jewish 'plunderers' very easy for themselves: three days previously members of Police Battalion 322 had already searched the Jewish quarter and designated all confiscated goods as 'plunder'.[40] Finally, during the massacre carried out by Police Battalions 316 and 322 in the middle of July in Bialystok about 3,000 Jewish men were killed.[41]

From the very beginning this gradual extension of the murders, partly on the initiative of the unit-leaders, partly on direct interventions by Himmler and senior SS officers, precisely corresponded to the open transmission of orders to the units. By using this procedure those responsible were supposed to grasp the essence of what was being demanded of them, and when necessary precise orders were added on site. In his meetings and instructions before the beginning of 'Barbarossa' Hitler had made certain of creating the appropriate climate for these orders to carry out murder. The murders were part of his conception of a war of racial extermination.

12

...SHOOT EVERYONE WHO EVEN LOOKS ODD

Extension of the Executions to Genocide,
Summer and Autumn 1941

After these murders had begun on a large scale, Hitler once again explicitly endorsed the brutal course that was being pursued. On 16 July 1941, at a conference with leading functionaries assigned to the Eastern territories at which the ground rules for the future policy of occupation were being established, he said, 'The vast area must naturally be pacified as quickly as possible; this will best be achieved by shooting everyone who even looks odd.'[1]

With the initiation of the mass murder of the Soviet civilian population in the summer of 1941, a stage had been reached by which these statements and similar ones by Hitler could no longer be understood as general threats of violence. The 'eliminatory' language of the dictator must be seen in the context of the mass murder that was now underway and that was being carried out by special units specially set up 'by special order of the Führer'. When Hitler now spoke of the 'extermination' (*Vernichtung*) of people, his subordinates must have understood it as it was intended: as direct or indirect instructions for the radicalisation of the mass murder already begun.

In accordance with this, the special units soon went on to extend their killings to women and children. This extension will be elaborated upon somewhat at this point, since it permits us to draw conclusions about the manner in which the instructions were given and about their nature. The way here was led by two SS brigades commanded directly by Himmler with the aid of a special staff. On 19 and 22 July these brigades were put at the disposal of the Higher SS and Police Leaders for Russia Centre and Russia South, Erich von dem Bach-Zelewski and Friedrich Jeckeln, Himmler's immediate subordinates in these areas.[2]

In the area behind the central section of the Front, it was the SS Cavalry Brigade that led the policy of extermination into a new stage with massacres of hitherto unparalleled scope. This Brigade carried out a first 'cleansing operation' in the Pripjet Marshes between 29 July and 23 August under the leadership of Bach-Zelewski, during which more than 25,000 Jews were shot.[3] Shortly before these two 'actions', Himmler had visited Baranovichi where he had issued the following order: 'All Jews must be shot. Jewish women to be driven into the marshes.'[4]

This order by Himmler introduced the escalation of the murders in the area of HSSPF Russia Centre: the Cavalry Brigade was indeed at first supposed to confine the killings to Jewish men, but the large number of their victims and Himmler's clear signal that women also were in future not to be spared had a radicalising effect on the operations of all units operational in this area.

Most of all this affected the units in the area for which the *Einsatzgruppe* (EG) B, deployed by Bach-Zelewski, was responsible. It can be proved that *Einsatzkommando* (EK) 9, shot women and children in the first half of August in Vileyka.[5] According to Alfred Filbert, the commander of EK 9, the order to shoot women and children had been given to him by Arthur Nebe, the commander of EG B.[6]

Otto Bradfisch, the commander of EK 8, also testified that in the first half of August he had received an order of the Führer's (*Führerbefehl*) from Nebe, which authorised the shooting of women and children[7] and which he had had confirmed personally by Himmler in Minsk in the middle of August.[8] The earliest point at which the indiscriminate shooting of women and children can be documented in the case of EK 8 is September, but it was intensified from October onwards. [9]

According to its own records, Police Battalion 322 had shot sixty-four Jewish women in Minsk on 1 September,[10] and on 25 September in the context of a 'demonstration exercise' (*Lehrübung*), the Battalion performed the formal searching of a village before representatives of the Wehrmacht, police and SD. During this 'exercise', nineteen Jewish women were murdered.[11]

It was only after this bloody demonstration that special units, the police, the civilian authorities, as well as local police, began indiscriminate massacres of men, women and children, thousands at a time, in Mogilev[12] Bobruisk, Borissov, Vitebsk and Gomel.[13] City by city, district by district, the entire Jewish population was systematically murdered, with the exception of a small number kept alive to serve as a workforce. EG B reported a total of 45,467 liquidations for their area by the end of October.[14]

The First SS Brigade, directly under the command of the HSSPF Russia South, Friedrich Jeckeln, moved on to the murder of Jewish women on the occasion of a 'cleansing action' at the end of July, on the explicit orders of Jeckeln.[15] According to the Brigade's own report 800 people, 'Jews and Jewesses between the ages of 16 and 60', were shot.[16] There followed further mass executions in which Jewish women were also shot.[17] At the end of August, the Brigade carried out a massacre in Kamenets-Podolsk which exceeded all previous 'actions'. According to the event-report of 22 August, after speaking to the Quartermaster-General of the Army,[18] 'in three days 23,600 Jews', men, women and children, 'were shot by one unit sent by the Höherer SS-und Polizeiführer [HSSPF]'.[19]

After this point, Jeckeln continued the massacres, in Berdichev[20] and in Zitomir[21] then with the murder of the Jews of Kiev in the gorge of Babi Yar,[22] and then in Dnepropetrovsk.[23] By the end of October, he had murdered more than 100,000 people.[24]

For the special units and police battalions that had been deployed in the south sector, and which had sometimes already been directly involved in the large 'actions' initiated by Jeckeln, these massacres represented the decisive impetus for a move to the comprehensive destruction of those Jewish populations.

From the beginning of August onwards, EK 4a murdered women in large numbers, and shortly afterwards murdered children too;[25] it extended these operations in the following weeks.[26] In September EK 5 murdered all the Jewish inhabitants of one town,[27] and according to information given by the unit commander, Erwin Schulz, he had been instructed to do this by Otto Rasch, the leader of EG C, who had himself received the order from Jeckeln.[28] EK 6 only began shooting Jewish women in October, which was in Krivoi Rog, after Himmler had been to visit it on 3 October.[29] Police Battalion 314 shot women and children as early as July,[30] Police Battalion 45 did the same from the end of July or early August onwards.[31] Both units were part of the Police Regiment South.

The shooting of women and children in the area of EG D is documented for the first time for the period at the end of August. On about 29 August, in the region of Jampol, EK 12 shot several hundred women, men and children,[32] and shortly thereafter, at least three, however possibly all four of the commandos of EG D proceeded to murder systematically the entire Jewish population of different villages.[33] The decisive order for the transition to this new stage of mass murder came at the end of August or the beginning of September from Otto Ohlendorf, according to testimony after the war by the commander of EK 12, Gustav Nosske, and one of his subordinates, Max Drexel.[34]

For the period between 30 September and 6 October there is documentary evidence that the Reichsführer SS made a tour of inspection in the Ukraine on which he visited Nikolayev and Cherson, where mass executions took place at that time or shortly thereafter.[35] And in the following months EG D continued this murderous process and reported whole areas 'free from Jews' (*judenfrei*).[36]

Finally there is EG A: EK 3 (stationed in Lithuania) and EK Tilsit made the transition to shooting women and children at the end of July or at the beginning of August,[37] EK 2 probably did so during the month of August.[38]

Taking all this together, we have the following picture: some units extended shooting to women and children as of the end of July 1941, but for others this began only in September or early October. Whilst for some units this extension to the murder of women and children was linked directly with murdering the entire Jewish population in certain districts, in the case of other units, the time-lag between these two levels of radicalisation was several weeks. Those Jews who had survived the first wave of murders (those needed by the Germans as workforces, for example), and those who were enclosed in ghettos, in September and October 1941 became victims of the ghetto liquidation measures that extended through the winter of 1941–42 into the entire year of 1942.

In order to force through this decisive stage of the radicalisation process, the orders given at the beginning of the war
had to be extended over the course of the summer. A reconstruction of the events leads to the conclusion that this was
not done by means of a single written order sent to all units
at the same time; repeated oral instructions must rather have
come from the SS leadership to the unit leaders, who were
then to take the initiative themselves and proceed more radically in their shooting programmes.

Important stages in this radicalisation process were
Himmler's oral instruction of 30 July to drive 'Jewish women
into the marshes' and his stay in Minsk on 15 August in which
he alluded to the imminent shootings of women and children. From statements made by different unit commanders it
is apparent that they were likewise encouraged by their superiors to shoot women and children in August and September
(Filbert and Bradfisch by Nebe, Schulz by Rasch, Nosske and
Drexel by Ohlendorf). It is also significant here that the
HSSPF Russia Centre and Russia South, who were immediate subordinates of Himmler's, took the decisive initiative: by
deploying the SS Brigades as well as by implementing 'major
actions' that brought together the EK, police battalions and
other units, they increased the numbers of victims to hitherto
unparalleled levels, killing women and children as well. In this
way, the direct participation in such 'actions' of a large number
of units in the centre and south districts encouraged them to
more radical steps. Repeatedly Himmler appeared at the
places concerned either shortly before or shortly after the
'major actions' in order to strengthen the members of the SS
and police in their murderous activities.

The extension of the shootings to women and children in
the summer and autumn of 1941, which had initiated the

murder of the entire Jewish civilian population in the occupied Soviet areas, was carried out by means of the 'indirect'
method of giving orders. The SS leadership gave a general
context for activity which the unit commanders had to fill in
using their own initiative and intuition.

It seems in fact that it was Himmler, the point at which the
various chains of command met, who took the decisive initiative in the extension of the murders of the Jewish civilian
population in the occupied Soviet zones. He did so after a
decisive meeting on 16 July, at which Hitler established the
basic outline of the occupation policy and recommended
'shooting everyone who even looks odd'.[39] Himmler was not
present at this summit meeting and was entrusted only with
using the police to secure the newly conquered Eastern
territories, not with the 'pacification and consolidation of
political matters' in these areas. This may have encouraged
him to extend of his own accord the authority and jurisdiction he already had. This he did in two ways. First, he extended
the mass shootings of Jews, whose victims had so far been
Jewish men of military age, who were all indiscriminately
suspected of being plunderers, communists or supporters of
the partisans, expanding the range of victims to include the
whole Jewish population. By extending what were at first
terrorist murder campaigns to the level of genocide, he put
into practice during the war itself a policy that the National
Socialist regime had originally planned for the time *after* the
war. According to the plans made by the regime,[40] the population of the Soviet Union was to be decimated, reduced by
some 30 million people, and it was self-evident for them that
the members of the Jewish minority were to be the first
victims of this policy. What had originally been, in their terms,
a utopian plan for the time after the end of the war was now

turned into concrete measures by Himmler, since the war could now not be won within a few months, as had been planned. The mass murder of the Jews was in his eyes the first step towards the 'new order', in racial terms, in the conquered territories.

The second way in which Himmler expanded his own sphere of authority was to extend his jurisdiction as Reichskommissar (Reich Commissioner for the consolidation of the German Volk) to the Soviet Union, without first being given explicit authority for this by Hitler. It should be borne in mind that as Reichskommissar Himmler was responsible not only for the settlement of German nationals but also, and especially, for the 'exclusion of damaging influences from [...] sectors of the population who were not truly part of the German Volk'. At the beginning of September, when the extension of the shootings to include women and children was fully underway, Hitler satisfied Himmler's wishes by declaring that the occupied Eastern territories now also fell under the jurisdiction of the Reichskommissar for the consolidation of the national character.[41] By extending the mass shootings, Himmler had therefore succeeded in expanding his responsibilities in the areas of the police and the 'Consolidation of the Volk' such that he was now taking a leading role in the racial 'new ordering' of the occupied areas.

At a later point, in a speech to the Reichsleiter and Gauleiter on 6 October 1943, and in a speech to the generals on 24 May 1944, Himmler was to use formulations that suggest that extending the murders to women and children was done on his initiative. He was to make it just as clear, however, that this decisive step was taken within the context of the policies authorised by Hitler. These speeches will be examined later.[42]

What has already been established for the manner in which orders were given within the SS and the Police apparatus will be true of Hitler's concrete instructions to Himmler: Hitler's instructions allowed him relatively wide scope for action. The Reichsführer SS was acting on the basis of general precepts and a general authority, on the basis in fact of a fundamental consensus. Much depended on his own initiative and on his own intuition, and he repeatedly made certain that his actions were in accord with Hitler's intentions.

The rabidly anti-Semitic tenor of Hitler's fundamental instructions for the war of racial destruction indicates his attitude. He did not only agree in principle with Himmler in the matter of the 'Jewish question', he validated his actions with his own authority and was fully informed of the murders in the Eastern territories.

The SS took no measures whatsoever to keep the mass murders in the East secret within the structures of power. The event-reports from the USSR — the main source of our information on these mass murders — had a relatively wide circulation. For example, forty-five copies of event-report no. 40 of 1 August 1941 were distributed; they were sent not only to numerous offices of the SS and the Police but also to the Leadership Staff of the Wehrmacht. In a radio telegram to the *Einsatzgruppen* on 1 August, Gestapo chief Müller, who was responsible for the compilation of event-reports, ordered that 'especially interesting visual material' should be sent to Berlin because 'the Führer is to be presented continuously with reports on the work of the *Einsatzgruppen* in the East from here'.[43] The distribution list of event-report no. 128 of 3 November 1941, of which there were fifty-five copies, included the Party Chancellery, which communicated between Hitler and the Party. A folder with the first six detailed activity- and situation-reports submitted by the *Einsatzgruppen* (July-October 1941) circulated in the Foreign Ministry and was initialled by no less than twenty-two civil servants.[44] It is therefore not possible to argue that the mass murders by the *Einsatzgruppen* were kept secret from other agencies by the *Reichssicherheitshauptamt* and there is no question that they were available to Hitler. The grounds for the mass executions given by the *Einsatzgruppen* correspond precisely with the justifications offered by Hitler for the extermination of the 'Jewish-Bolshevik complex' before the beginning of the war, and once again they express the fundamental conformity of outlook on the 'Jewish question' between Hitler and the SS leadership.

13

IT IS GOOD IF THE TERROR THAT WE ARE EXTERMINATING THE JEWS GOES BEFORE US

The Start of Deportations, Autumn 1941

In the middle of September 1941 Hitler ordered the deportation of the Jews from the Greater German Reich into ghettos in Eastern Europe. He thereby set in motion the deportation plans which he had pursued at the beginning of 1941, without waiting for the original precondition – the military victory over the Red Army. Only a month earlier, in the middle of August, Hitler had spoken against 'evacuations' of Jews from Germany.[1]

At the same point, the middle of August, he had, however, explained to the Minister for Propaganda that he had not given up his plans relating to this matter:

> We were talking about the Jewish problem. The Führer is convinced that the prophecy he made in the Reichstag – that if the Jews succeeded in provoking another world war he would finish by destroying the Jews – is now being confirmed. It is coming true in these weeks and months with almost uncanny certainty. In the East the Jews have had to settle their account; in Germany they have partly settled and will have to pay even more in future.[2]

On 18 September 1941 Himmler informed Greiser, the Gauleiter in the Warthegau, of the following:

> The Führer would like the Altreich and the Protectorate from the West to the East to be emptied and liberated of Jews as

soon as possible. As a first stage, I am therefore trying – hope-fully this year still – to transport the Jews of the Altreich and those from the Protectorate into the Eastern territories that have been newly absorbed into the Reich in the last two years; this is in order to push them further East in the coming spring.

I intend to place about 60,000 Jews from the Altreich and the Protectorate in the Litzmannstadt [Lodz] ghetto, which I understand has enough room to accommodate them, for the winter.[3]

In the following weeks Hitler repeatedly confirmed his deter-mination to deport the Jews from Central Europe to the East. On 6 October he announced to his lunch guests as he described proposed penalties against the Czechs that all Jews from the Protectorate must be 'removed' (*entfernt*), not just sent to the Generalgouvernement Poland but rather 'imme-diately sent further away, to the East'.[4] According to Hitler, however, this was not possible at the moment, because of the shortage of transport capacity. At the same time as the 'Protectorate Jews', the Jews were also to 'disappear' (*ver-schwinden*) from Vienna and Berlin.

On 25 October Hitler made the following remark at table, after he had once again made mention of his 'prophecy' of 30 January 1939:

This criminal race has the two million dead from the World War on its conscience, now hundreds of thousands more. No one can say to me: we can't send them into the morass! Who then cares about our people? It is good if the terror that we are exterminating the Jews goes before us.[5]

The deportations from Germany did in fact begin on 15 October 1941.[6] Why did Hitler at this point take the decision to start on deportations that he had been planning since early 1941, even though the war was not yet won? Leading functionaries of the regime were demanding these measures. Amongst others, the Reich Minister for the Occupied Eastern Territories, Rosenberg, had suggested deportations in September as a reaction to Stalin's decision to deport the Volga Germans to the East.[7] At this point, too, several Gauleiter were demanding that Jews be pushed out of their living areas in order to create housing for those affected by the bombing raids.[8] For Hitler it seems that yet another motive played a role: by deporting the Central European Jews he wanted to send a warning to 'world Jewry' (*das Weltjudentum*) – in the sense of his 'prophecy' of 30 January 1939 – and thereby prevent the entry of the United States into the war. The leadership of the USA, in his opinion, was a puppet of 'world Jewry', a theme that was particularly conspicuous in German propaganda in the following few weeks.[9]

Hitler's motives become apparent from a memo written on 20 September by Werner Koeppen, the representative for the Eastern Ministry in Hitler's headquarters. Koeppen wrote that Ambassador Steengracht (representative of the Foreign Office in the headquarters of the Führer) had told him that Hitler was considering the question of postponing possible reprisals (*Pressalien*) against the German Jews 'for the eventuality of an American entry into the war'.[10] One of the motives for the deportations of October 1941, which took place openly and were registered by the international press, was thus also the idea of using the Jews as hostages. This motive had also been involved in the projects of a 'Jewish reservation' in Poland and a police government on Madagascar.

These different motives for the implementation of the deportations appear secondary however, when one remembers that from the beginning of his political career Hitler had intended to get rid of the Jews within the German *Lebensraum* in one way or another and had pressed forward with plans for mass deportation from the very beginning of the war. With the conquest of the enormous Soviet area it seemed to him for the first time that a practical possibility was available for the realisation of these plans.

Hitler's decision in September to deport the Jews from Central Europe did not yet include the resolution immediately and systematically to murder them at their destinations in occupied Poland and the Soviet territory (especially Lodz, Riga and Minsk). Evidently Hitler initially clung to the idea of deporting these people further to the East once the expected military victory over the Soviet Union had been achieved.[11]

On 24 September, after a meeting with Heydrich on the previous day, Goebbels wrote in his diary, 'we must evacuate the Jews from Berlin as soon as possible'.[12] He added that:

this will be possible as soon as we have cleared up the military situation in the East. In the end, they should all be transported [to the] camps set up [by the] Bolsheviks. These camps have been constructed by the Jews; what would be more apt now than to have them peopled by the Jews.

At a meeting in Prague two weeks later on 10 October, where Eichmann was also present, Heydrich said the following:[13]

There are at this time about 88,000 Jews in the Protektorat as a whole, 48,000 of whom are in Prague. [...] There have been difficulties because of the evacuations. It was intended to begin on or around 15 October, and to roll out the transports gradually until 15 November, up to the level of about 5,000 Jews – from Prague alone. [...] Minsk and Riga are to receive 50,000. [...] In the coming weeks the 5,000 Jews are to be evacuated from Prague. SS-Brigadeführer Nebe and Rasch could take Jews into the camps for communist prisoners in the operational area.[14] According to SS-Sturmbannführer Eichmann, this measure has already been initiated. [...] The Gypsies to be evacuated could be brought to Stahlecker in Riga, whose camp is operated along the lines of the one in Sachsenhausen. As the Führer wishes the Jews to be brought out of German territory by the end of the year if possible, all unsettled questions must be solved immediately.

In a first wave of deportations between 15 October and 5 November, 10,000 Jews from the Altreich, 5,000 each from the Protektorat and Vienna, and 5,000 Gypsies from the Austrian Burgenland, were deported to Lodz[15] in twenty-four transports. Between 8 November 1941 and 6 February 1942, altogether thirty-four different transports went to Riga,[16] Kovno[17] and Minsk[18] Originally this wave of deportations was to have been stopped by the beginning of December, and was to encompass the deportation of 50,000 people.[19] The deportations to Minsk, however, had to be broken off at the end of November due to problems of transportation. By then approximately 8,000 people had been deported into the Minsk ghetto. The transports to Riga were completed at the end of February, having fulfilled the planned quota of 25,000 people.[20]

However, in autumn 1941 the RHSA's plans for deportations extended beyond Central Europe and were aimed at the whole territory under German domination. We can tell from a statement made by Heydrich that at the same time as, or shortly after his decision taken in mid-September to deport the Jews of Central Europe, Hitler took the more far-reaching decision to make preparations for the deportation of all the Jews in territories under German rule. In a letter to the General Quartermaster of the Army of 6 November 1941, Heydrich defended his explicit assent to the attacks on seven synagogues in Paris that had been perpetrated by a group of French anti-Semites in the night of 2-3 November. The suggestion to carry out this attack, according to Heydrich, was:

> accepted by me only at the point where the Jews were identified on the highest authority and most vehemently as being those responsible for setting Europe alight, and who must ultimately disappear from Europe.[21]

A further indication in favour of a decision to extend the deportations across the whole of occupied Europe that was taken in September 1941 is the activity of the 'Jewish expert' in the German Embassy in Paris, Carltheo Zeitschel.[22] Through the intervention of Abetz, the Ambassador in Paris, Zeitschel succeeded in securing Himmler's fundamental approval for the eastward deportation of the foreign Jews interned in France.[23] This was in mid-September 1941, that is at exactly the time Hitler had decided to start the deportations from Germany. (In his proposal Zeitschel had taken it for granted that the removal of this group represented only the first step in the deportation of all Jews under German domination to the occupied Eastern Territories).[24] In autumn 1941, the German military administration in occupied France fell in line with Zeitschel's proposal of mid-September. As a reprisal for attacks by the French Resistance, it decided to

deport a large number of Jews and communists, who had
been arrested in mass raids in May and August 1941[25], and
send them 'to the East' to carry out forced labour.[26]
From December 1941 onward, Jews and communists were
singled out by name for these deportations. These 'hostage-
deportations', although initially put back by transportation
problems, eventually started operation in March 1942.[27]

There are a few other indicators that the deportation of all
European Jews was being planned as early as autumn 1941. In
a meeting with representatives of the Ministry for the
Occupied Eastern territories on 4 October, Heydrich indicated the possibility of companies claiming Jewish workers.
This, however, 'would destroy the plan of a total evacuation
of Jews from the occupied territories'.[28]

Also the Head of the Jewish desk of the Foreign Office,
Franz Rademacher, still assumed at the end of October 1941
that the Serbian Jews who had survived the repressive measures of the Wehrmacht, would be 'removed by ship into the
transition camps in the East.'[29] This was to happen as soon as
'the technical feasibility within the general framework of the
comprehensive solution to the Jewish Question' was established.

Was the deportation of Jews 'to the East' at this time already
a metaphor for their planned murder in the extermination
camps? The current state of research does not offer sufficient
evidence for this conclusion.[30] Until early 1942, in fact, neither the Central European nor the French Jews were sent
directly to extermination camps. Furthermore, these camps
were not significantly expanded until early 1942 and early
summer 1942. Until the contrary has been proven, one should
thus take the statements of leading Nazis literally – that the
intention behind the deportations and the planning of

autumn 1941 was still to deport all European Jews to camps in the occupied Soviet Union, after victory had been achieved.

The RSHA's programme of deportations for German Jews, and their broader plans for the deportation of Jews throughout the area under German control, were secured by a number of administrative measures. On 1 September 1941 German Jews were required by police decree to wear the 'yellow star' with the word 'Jew' on it,[31] after Hitler had given his express consent to a suggestion of this nature made by Goebbels a few days previously.[32]

At the beginning of November 1941 the German Finance Ministry issued regulations concerning the acquisition of the wealth owned by 'Jews who are to be moved in the coming months to a city in the Eastern zone'.[33] This procedure was considerably simplified by the eleventh decree pertaining to the *Reichsbürgergesetz* (German citizenship law) passed on 25 November.[34] The effects of this were that the Jews deported to the East lost their German citizenship when they crossed the German border and everything they owned immediately became the possession of Germany.[35]

Finally, on 23 October a decree of the RHSA in Himmler's name prohibited the emigration of all Jews from the whole area under German rule.[36] The decision to take this step was made by the RHSA in the middle of October. It was prompted by information from the Foreign Ministry to the effect that Spanish Jews living in France were intending to leave for Spanish Morocco. The RHSA opposed this move 'because of the measures that are to be taken after the end of the war towards a final solution of the Jewish question'.[37] The decision to ban emigration was therefore taken at precisely the same time as the deportation of Jews from Germany began. It was a decisive precondition for the implementation of the plan, still current, which envisaged the total deportation of all Jews in areas under German domination into the occupied Eastern territories after the end of the war.

Immediately after issuing the ban on emigration, in November, the Foreign Ministry asked the governments of Slovakia, Croatia and Rumania if they had any objections to the deportation of their Jewish citizens residing in Germany. All three governments replied that they had no objection.[38]

14

WE ARE EXPERIENCING THE FULFILMENT OF THIS PROPHECY

The Extension of Mass Murder in Autumn 1941

P arallel to the beginning of the deportations, the transfer of gas-killing technology into the Eastern European regions began from September and October 1941 onwards. This technology had been under development in the context of the 'euthanasia programme' since 1939.

The transfer was initiated after the programme of 'euthanasia' had been stopped in August 1941. The so-called 'euthanasia programme', which had been planned in 1939, had involved the murder of approximately 20 per cent of all inmates of psychiatric institutions in Germany. Altogether more than 70,000 people had been killed in the framework of the so-called 'Operation T4' (*Aktion* T4) when it was brought to an end.[1] Only a few weeks later, the first preparations can be documented for the construction of gas chambers in Eastern Europe.

The decision to build the first extermination camp in Belzec was made in mid-October 1941.[2] The killing was to proceed using exhaust gases from a permanently installed motor. Construction started at the beginning of November, and the murder experts from 'Operation T4' were ordered to Belzec in December 1941.

Likewise in October 1941, the Chancellery of the Führer, which was responsible for 'Operation T4', began preparations for building gas chambers in Riga. This is clear from a document in which Erhard Wetzel, the specialist for racial questions in the Ministry for the occupied Eastern territories, offered Reichskommisar Heinrich Lohse, who was in charge of the former Baltic States and White Russia, 'gassing apparatus' that was to be put at his disposal by the Chancellery of the Führer.[3] Gas chambers were not in fact erected in Riga. Instead, so-called 'gas vans' were employed.

These gas vans were developed by the Criminal Police in autumn 1941.[4] After a first attempt in which mentally ill patients were killed using engine exhaust gases in an asylum in Mogilew in September 1941,[5] the RSHA took the decision that its *Einsatzgruppen* (or task-forces) would use mobile gas chambers. The SK Lange (Lange Special Unit) had already used such vehicles in winter 1939/40 to murder asylum inmates in Poland. Now, however, instead of using carbon-monoxide gas bottles, as previously, the exhaust of the vehicles was pumped directly into the passenger-carriage.[6] At the beginning of November 1941, the first 'test' of such a vehicle took place in Sachsenhausen. About thirty prisoners were killed by exhaust fumes.[7] In the occupied Soviet territories, the gas vans were first used to kill people in November or early December. By the end of 1941 gas vans were in use by all four task-forces.[8]

At around the same time, from October or November 1941 onwards, the gas vans were also deployed by the special unit SK Lange in the Warthegau to murder Jews. On 8 December the killing began in Chelmno, where gas vans were established permanently – a further variant of an extermination camp.[9]

While the mass murders using exhaust gases were being prepared or had already been committed in Belzec, the Warthegau and in the occupied Eastern territories, the Commandant of the Auschwitz concentration camp took another course. In September or December 1941, 600 Soviet

prisoners of war and 250 selected sick prisoners were murdered in the basement of Block 11 of Auschwitz by means of
a high concentration of the extremely poisonous disinfectant
Zyklon B. At a later point, in December 1941, a further 900
Soviet prisoners of war were murdered using poisonous gas.[10]

Writing in Cracow prison after the war, the former
Commandant of Auschwitz, Rudolf Höß, described how the
question of the most suitable poison-gas to be employed had
been discussed on the occasion of a visit by Eichmann.[11] The
date of this visit is still not certain – some of his comments
indicate the autumn of 1941, others point to a later date, perhaps spring 1942. Höß further states that during the time that
he was not in Auschwitz himself, his deputy used Zyklon B
on his own initiative to kill Soviet prisoners of war.[12]

In November 1941, Topf & Söhne of Erfurt, a company
specialising in the construction of crematoria, received the
assignment to build an enormous 32-chamber furnace in
Mogilev, White Russia. This installation was needed – so the
company was told – to dispose of corpses hygienically because
of the great danger of epidemics in the East. As the construction was not completed, the ovens which were no
longer needed went to Auschwitz.[13] It is possible that this
crematorium installation was in fact planned as part of an
extermination camp in Mogilev, whose function was taken
over by Auschwitz and the Polish extermination camps in the
following months.[14]

Thus, at the end of 1941, preparations were underway for
the construction of extermination camps not only in
Auschwitz, but also in Riga, in the area of Lodz (Chelmno),
in Belzec and presumably also in Mogilev, that is, in the area
of Minsk, thus in the proximity of all the ghettos that had
been chosen as the destinations for the first to third waves of

deportations from the Greater German Reich.[15] The parallels in timing between the beginning of the deportations and the preparation and installation of the murder-machinery reflect the plan of the Nazi regime to extend the strategy of 'Jew-free' (*judenfrei*) areas – already implemented in the Soviet Union – to the Polish territories. In certain regions of central importance for the arrangements for the displacement of people in the racist 'New Order', the elimination of those elements of the local Jewish population who were 'unfit for work' was the minimum requirement. In the preceding months, attempts on all sides to develop or improve on technologies of mass killing using gas are clear indications of comprehensive preparations to extend the scale of mass murder in the near future. (In the case of Auschwitz these preparations were concerned with Soviet POWs and the sick, and not yet primarily with Jewish prisoners).[16] However, at this time plans for the systematic mass murder of the Jewish population only extended to certain regions. At the same time, though, the intention was still to deport the remaining Jews to the occupied Soviet territories after the war.

In autumn 1941 regional murders of some parts of the Jewish population were not only carried out in the Warthegau and the district of Lublin, where deportation trains from Germany were expected, but also in the district of Galicia, part of the Generalgouvernement Poland and in Serbia. By the end of 1941 these four regions give a picture as follows. In the Warthegau, after Hitler's decision of mid-September 1941 to begin with the deportations of Jews from the Greater German Reich, the first deportation trains began to arrive. 20,000 Jews and 5,000 Gypsies were enclosed in the ghetto at Lodz, which was already filled to over-capacity. At about the same time, probably still in October 1941, the mass murder of local Jews began in the area of Konin in the southern Warthegau.[17] In an 'action' lasting several days at the end of November, 700 Jews were killed in gas vans at the camp of Bornhagen (Kozminek) in the area of Kalisch.[18] This was carried out by the SK Lange, which had already murdered thousands of mental asylum inmates in gas vans in the annexed Polish regions in 1939/40 and in June/July 1941.[19] In October 1941, Lange's unit was called to Novgorod by Himmler in order to kill the patients of mental asylums there.[20] Lange's driver testified that he had been told to chauffeur Lange around the Warthegau in the autumn of 1941 in order to find a suitable place for a stationary murder-installation. After a suitable building had been found in Chelmno, Lange's unit started killing Jews there, using gas vans, on 8 December. At first, it was mainly local Jews who had been deported from various areas of the Warthegau to Chelmno that were killed. From January 1942 onward, however, it was predominantly Polish Jews from the ghetto of Lodz who were put to death at Chelmno.[21]

A letter to Himmler from Greiser, governor of the Warthegau, dated 1 May 1942 gives important evidence for the reconstruction of the decision to carry out the mass murder of Jews in the Warthegau.[22] In this letter Greiser writes that the 'special treatment of around 100,000 Jews in my district [which was] authorised by you in agreement with the Head of the *Reichsichterheitshauptamt* SS Obergruppen-führer Heydrich' could be 'completed in the next 2-3 months'. If Himmler and Heydrich had to 'authorise' this mass murder, then it is to be assumed that this suggestion was made by Greiser himself.[23] The murder of the 100,000 people (Polish Jews 'unfit for work') was hence presumably the 'quid pro quo' that Greiser had demanded of Himmler to take approx-

imately 25,000 Jews and Gypsies (instead of the 60,000 originally proposed by Himmler) into the ghetto of Lodz in
October and November 1941.

From spring 1941, the authorities in the Generalgouvernement Poland had been working under the
assumption that the Jews in their area would be deported to
the conquered Soviet areas in the near future. In a private
conversation of 13 October 1941, Frank renewed his suggestion to Rosenberg to deport 'the Jewish population of the
Generalgouvernement Poland into the occupied Eastern
Territories'. Rosenberg responded that there was no possibility of the 'implementation of such resettlement-plans' at the
moment. For the future, however, Rosenberg expressed his
willingness to 'promote Jewish emigration to the East, especially seeing that there is the intention to send all asocial
elements of the Reich to the thinly inhabited Eastern
Territories'.[24] From this point onward, the authorities in the
Generalgouvernement Poland began to think about a 'final
solution' to the 'Jewish Question' on its own territory.

A series of meetings of the leadership of the Generalgouvernement Poland was of great consequence for the
general radicalisation of policy with respect to the Jews in
this area. These were arranged in the district capitals by Frank,
immediately following his return from Germany (14-16
October in Warsaw, 17 October in Globocnik's district of
Lublin, 18 October in Radom, 20 October in Cracow, and
for the first time in Lvov, 21 October). At the meeting in
Lublin on 17 October, the 'Third Regulation Concerning
Restrictions on the Right of to Reside in the
Generalgouvernement Poland' was discussed. This regulation
introduced the death penalty for leaving the ghetto and
was issued only a few days later.[25] On 20 October, at the

government meeting in Cracow, Governor Wächter indicated 'that an ultimately radical solution to the 'Jewish Question' is unavoidable, and that no allowances of any kind – such as special exceptions for craftsmen – could be taken into consideration.'[26] At the meeting on 21 October in Lvov, Eberhard Westerkamp, the Head of the Department for the Interior in the Generalgouvernement Poland, announced, that 'the isolation of the Jews from the rest of the population' should be enforced 'as soon and as thoroughly as possible'. On the other hand, he pointed out that 'the government order has prohibited the establishment of new ghettos, since there was hope that the Jews would be deported from the Generalgouvernement Poland in the near future', even though Rosenberg had unambiguously shattered this 'hope' a few days previously.[27]

While the treatment of the 'Jewish Question' at these meetings indicated that the leadership of the Generalgouvernement Poland was pursuing a unified anti-Jewish policy throughout the region under its control, two districts took the lead in the implementation of the 'final solution'.

An important factor in the preparations for the 'final solution' in the Generalgouvernement Poland was the fact that Galicia was absorbed into its territory on 1 August: this was an area in which mass executions of Jews had taken place on a large scale since the beginning of the war against the Soviet Union and were continuing. The special commando unit EG z.b.V. (which had been deployed in this area and became the office of the Commander of the Security Police in the District of Galicia once Galicia had joined the Generalgouvernement Poland) focussed its operations first against a vaguely defined Jewish elite.[28] From the beginning of October, however, the Security Police began to kill members of the Jewish population indiscriminately in Galicia as well. On 6 October in Nadvorna, about 2,000 men, women and children were murdered by members of the Stanislau outpost of the Commander of the Security Police in Galicia.[29] According to a statement made by Hans Krüger, the Chief of the Security Police in Stanislau, this 'action' had been planned down to the last detail at a meeting with the Commander of the Security Police in Lemberg.[30] From the beginning of October, massacres of this type were carried out almost every week. One that deserves special notice was the so-called 'Blood Sunday of Stanislau', 12 October 1941, when between 10,000–12,000 Jews were murdered.[31] The Security Police in Galicia were thus following the same pattern of radicalisation as the units in the occupied Eastern areas, independently of the political subordination of the district. These mass executions necessarily radicalised the anti-Jewish policy throughout the Generalgouvernement Poland.

Concrete preparations for the mass murder of Jews in the Generalgouvernement Poland had also been underway since October in the district of Lublin that bordered on Galicia. This was the territory which had been planned for a 'Jewish reservation' in 1939 and which in spring 1942 was to serve as a receiving area for the third wave of deportations from Germany, as well as for deportations from Slovakia.

The SS and Police Commander of the district of Lublin, Odilo Globocnik, played a key role in the murder of Jews in this district. On 13 October, Globocnik met Himmler[32] to speak to him about the proposal that he had made two weeks earlier to limit the 'influence of the Jews' against whom it was necessary to take steps 'of a security policy nature'.[33] It was presumably at this meeting that Globocnik received the assignment to build the Belzec extermination camp, since at the beginning of November, two to three weeks after this meeting and after the 'Jewish Question' had been discussed by the leadership of the Generalgouvernement Poland at several meetings, work began on the construction of Belzec, which was a relatively small group of barracks.[34] By the end of the year, the delegated euthanasia personnel of the 'T4 Organisation' had arrived in Lublin.[35]

The killing capacity of Belzec was still relatively limited at this point (it was to be considerably expanded early the following year), and the construction of the remaining extermination camps in the Generalgouvernement Poland did not begin until early 1942. These facts indicate that by autumn 1941 Globocnik had not, as yet, received the order to prepare for the killing of all Jews in the Generalgouvernement Poland and that his assignment only encompassed the district of Lublin, and possibly also the district of Galicia.[36]

Alongside the events in the Generalgouvernement Poland and the Warthegau a further sequence of regional mass murders began in October 1941, namely the systematic murder of the Jewish men in Serbia. From the beginning of July 1941 onwards the German military administration had hostages, communists and Jews shot almost daily to 'avenge' acts of resistance.[37] In August, arrests were extended to all Jewish men. As was already the case in the Soviet Union, the 'avenging measures' in Serbia were thus directed against the image of the enemy as a 'Jewish Bolshevist'. Despite the shootings, the Serbian resistance to the occupying power continued to grow. After twenty-two German soldiers were killed in an ambush, the General in command in Serbia, Hans-Joachim Böhme, ordered on 4 October 'the immediate shooting of 100 Serbian prisoners for each German soldier killed', as 'a reprisal and an atonement'.[38] Those to be executed were prisoners of the concentration camps in Sabac and Belgrade, 'principally Jews and communists'.[39] About 2,000 Jews and 200 Gypsies from these concentration camps were killed between 9 and 13 October.[40] Böhme's policy of directing his 'avenging measures' against Jews in the first instance had influential support: in a letter of 16 September Martin Luther, the Head of the German Department of the Foreign Office, had directed the representative of the Foreign Office in Belgrade to treat all imprisoned Jewish men as hostages,[41] and on 13 October 1941 Eichmann had recommended that the entire group of persons in question should be shot.[42]

On 10 October, Böhme issued the general command 'to shoot 100 prisoners or hostages for every German soldier or ethnic German (men, women or children) killed or murdered', and to shoot '50 prisoners or hostages for every wounded German soldier or ethnic German'. To be arrested as hostages 'at once' were 'all Communists, all male inhabitants suspected of being Communists, all Jews, a certain number of nationalist and democratically minded inhabitants'.[43]

In accordance with this scheme, a further 2,200 men were shot a few days later, Jews and Gypsies once more among them.[44] In the two weeks following the order of 10 October, Wehrmacht units shot more than 9,000 Jews, Gypsies and other civilians.[45] By the beginning of November, 8,000 Jewish men had been executed by the firing squads.[46] The families of those murdered were interned in concentration camps during the winter and murdered the following spring, in gas vans.[47]

Despite this rapid increase in mass murders, it should be observed that in autumn 1941, the mass murders and the preparations for wide-ranging killing campaigns were restricted to the Jewish population in the newly conquered former Soviet districts, to the Warthegau, now annexed, to the districts of Lublin and Galicia in the Generalgouvernement Poland and to Serbia.

After a total of 5,000 people from five transport trains arriving from Germany had been shot in November 1941 in Kovno on the instructions of the local offices of the security police,[48] Himmler ordered Heydrich by telephone on 30 November not to shoot 1,000 Berlin Jews who were already on a transport destined for Riga.[49] This order arrived too late, however, and the Berlin Jews had already been murdered. The fact that Himmler reprimanded Jeckeln, who was the HSSPF in charge and responsible for the shootings, and instructed him in future to keep to the 'guidelines' of the RSHA for the treatment of the Jews deported from Central Europe,[50] clearly shows that Jeckeln had acted on his own authority. The shooting of Jews from the area of the Greater German Reich was not authorised at this point. It is important to remember that in September 1941 Hitler had spoken of reserving reprisals against Central European Jews for the event that the USA entered the war.[51]

Whilst these regional mass murders were being perpetrated or prepared, in autumn 1941 there was an increasing number of statements being made by leading representatives of the regime that openly addressed the question of the 'annihilation' (*Vernichtung*) of the Jews that was to come. In a leading article for the journal *Das Reich* of 16 November 1941, Goebbels returned to the subject of Hitler's 'prophecy' of 30 January 1939 under the title 'The Jews are to Blame' (*Die Juden sind schuld*):

We are now experiencing the fulfilment of this prophecy, and Jewry is suffering a fate that, although hard, is still more than deserved. Here compassion or regret is completely amiss.

When he said 'world Jewry is now [undergoing] a gradual process of extermination', with this formulation Goebbels made clear the fate which was awaiting the Jews who were being deported from German cities over the past few weeks. Two days later, Rosenberg spoke at a press conference of the Ministry of the Eastern Territories of what was to come – the 'eradication' (*Ausmerzung*) of the Jews of Europe:

> There are still about six million Jews in the East and this question can only be solved through a biological eradication of all of European Jewry. The Jewish Question will only be solved for Germany when the last Jew has left German territory, and for Europe when there is no longer a Jew left standing on the European continent as far as the Urals. [...] And for this it is necessary to push them beyond the Urals, or otherwise eradicate them.[52]

Whilst it is true that extending the murders to particular areas outside the Soviet Union in the autumn of 1941 was done in the context of the deportation programmes ordered by Hitler, no-one has yet been able to find a direct order for the execution of these new mass murders or for the use of poison-gas. However, it can be indirectly demonstrated that Hitler gave the authorisation of these new mass murders, by looking at the sequence of events.

Looking at the events of autumn 1941 as a whole, it becomes evident that institutions with regional responsibility, were each, in a systematic manner, attempting to kill a substantial proportion of the Jewish population in their areas with the help of a particular method of murder. In the Warthegau the initiative lay with Gauleiter Greiser, who had been authorised by Himmler to murder 100,000 persons and did so with the help of gas vans. The preparations for the murder of Jews 'incapable of work' in the districts of Galicia and Lublin lay in the hands of Globocnik, the SS and Police Commandant of Lublin. In Serbia it was first the Wehrmacht that carried out mass executions of Jewish men and later the initiative passed to the Security Police, who killed the remainder of the Jewish population using gas vans. In every case, what was being carried out was a planned programme of annihilation. These regional annihilation programmes cannot be seen in isolation as independently running campaigns that had been started on the initiative of the regional authorities. They were instead components of a supra-regional policy that was being guided centrally.

As has been pointed out several times, the mass murders in the Warthegau and the district of Lublin were carried out in the context of a comprehensive deportation programme that initially affected only Germany, but whose extension to the whole of Europe had already been anticipated. The regional murder campaigns were designed to create 'room' for the first waves of deportees in the regions. Greiser and Globocnik were therefore not acting autonomously but had first to seek the agreement of Himmler before they could proceed with the mass murders in Chelmno and Belzec. As we have seen, the extension of these murders to the districts of Galicia and Lublin was a process that actively involved the civil administration of the Generalgouvernement Poland. The policy of extermination in Serbia was not a unique or isolated development but corresponded to German policy in the occupied Soviet areas, put back a little chronologically. Wehrmacht commander Böhme began with the execution of Jewish men only when the relevant positive instructions from the RHSA and the Foreign Ministry had been received. The mass executions in Galicia were again at first a component of the policy of annihilation in the occupied Soviet areas; later, with the deportations to Belzec, the same methods of murder were used here as had been used in the neighbouring district of Lublin.

An important feature common to all four regions (Warthegau, Lublin, Galicia and Serbia) is the use of gas to murder people. This method of murder fitted into a higher-level policy that can also be demonstrated to have operated in winter 1941-42 in Auschwitz (Zyklon B) and in the occupied Soviet areas (gas vans).

There was not only a close correlation between the deportations, the transfer of gas-technology and the beginnings of the murders in the regions; the execution of these complex operations involved a whole series of organisations outside the SS and the Police, such as the Reichsstatthalter in the Warthegau, the civil administration of the General-gouvernement Poland, the Foreign Ministry, the Wehrmacht and the Chancellery of the Führer. An operation of this magnitude could only be carried out in the Third Reich if it was covered by the authority of the Führer himself: he alone, as head of government, leader of the Nazi Party and commander-in-chief of the armed forces had the authority to give instructions to all the offices involved. Whether we should conceive of such authorisation as a single instruction, as a series of orders or as the general empowerment of one of his subordinates (Himmler, for example), and whether the initiative for the policy came from him in the first instance or from someone else – these questions cannot be settled. This does not, however, absolve Hitler from responsibility for the extension of the mass murders, as is emphasised by the following events.

15

THE WORLD WAR IS HERE, THE EXTERMINATION OF THE JEWS MUST BE THE NECESSARY CONSEQUENCE

The Radicalisation of Anti-Jewish Policy in December 1941

With the declaration of war against the USA on 11 December 1941 the concept of taking the West and Central European Jews 'hostage' became obsolete. At this point the 'final solution' – the systematic murder of all European Jews – was introduced and Hitler's central role in this last stage of escalation can once again be demonstrated.

On 12 December, one day after declaring war on the USA, Hitler gave a speech to the Party's Gauleiter and Reichleiter. Referring once more to his 'prophecy' of 30 January 1939, he announced the 'extermination' (*Vernichtung*) of the Jews under German domination, as Goebbels' diaries show:

> As far as the Jewish question is concerned, the Führer is deter-mined to make a clean sweep. He prophesied to the Jews that if they once again brought about a world war they would expe-rience their own extermination. This was not just an empty phrase. The World War is here, the extermination of the Jews must be the necessary consequence. This question must be seen without sentimentality. We are not here in order to show sym-pathy with the Jews, we must sympathise with our own German people. If the German people has now once again sacrificed as many as 160,000 lives in the Eastern campaign, then the authors of this bloody conflict must pay with their lives.[1]

Rosenberg, the German Minster for the occupied Eastern territories, reported in his diary that on 14 December he showed Hitler the manuscript for an address he was planning to give in Berlin. Rosenberg, who in a press conference of 18 November had openly spoken of a 'biological eradication (*Ausmerzung*) of the entirety of Jewry',[2] was now 'after the decision' (i.e. after the declaration of war on the United States) uncertain as to whether his planned 'remarks about Jews of New York did not perhaps [...] have to be somewhat altered.' He wrote:

> I took the view that I should not speak about the extirpation [*Ausrottung*] of the Jews. The Führer agreed with this attitude and said they had saddled us with the war and they had brought about the destruction; no wonder that they are the first to feel the consequences.[3]

Rosenberg's uncertainty was therefore related to representation of the 'extirpation' in propaganda and not to the fact itself, about which he and Hitler were in agreement.

On 18 December, Himmler noted the following key words in his appointments diary regarding a conversation with Hitler: 'Jewish question | to be extirpated [*auszurotten*] as partisans'.[4] It is evident from this note that Hitler was expressly confirming to Himmler that he should continue and intensify the mass murder of the Soviet Jews, which by then had cost several hundreds of thousands of lives, using the same pretext as before.[5] This memo is thus significant proof of the direct and fundamental participation of Hitler in the decision-making process concerning the mass murder of the Jews.

The deportations that resumed on a large scale in the spring of 1942, after the Wannsee Conference of 20 January, were preceded in January and February 1942 by a series of public declarations by Hitler in which he unambiguously returned to his 'prophecy' of January 1939, according to which the Jews of Europe would be exterminated if there was a new world war. Both the recent entry of the USA into the war (whereby the war had been extended into a world war), and the fact that in his statements Hitler continually assigned the date of 1 September 1939 to his prophecy, underlined his threat in a particular manner.

Accordingly in his New Year address, Hitler said, 'the Jew will not extirpate the peoples of Europe, he will be the victim of his own attack'.[6] In his address in the Sportpalast (the infamous assembley hall in Berlin where Hitler made many speeches) to commemorate 30 January, Hitler exclaimed, 'we are clear that the war can only end either if the Aryan peoples are extirpated or if Jewry disappears from Europe.'[7] In a statement read on 24 February 1942 in the Munich Hofbräuhaus, on the twenty-second anniversary of the founding of the Nazi Party, Hitler once again had the statement made (he was not present) to say, 'my prophecy will find its fulfilment in that through this war it will not be that Aryan mankind will be exterminated, but that the Jew will be extirpated.'[8] Hitler expressed himself similarly in a smaller circle, among members of his entourage and private guests: 'The Jew must get out of Europe! It would be best if they went to Russia! I have no sympathy with the Jews. They will always remain an element which stir up the peoples against one another.'[9] And in February 1942:

> The Jew will be identified! The same battle that Pasteur and Koch had to fight must be led by us today. Innumerable sicknesses have their origin in one bacillus: the Jew! Japan would also have got it had it remained open any longer to the Jew. We will get well when we eliminate the Jews.[10]

On 14 February he said to Goebbels that he was determined:

> to be quite ruthless to clear out the Jews in Europe. There was
> no place here for an access of sentimentality. The Jews have
> fully deserved the catastrophe that they are facing today. They
> will also experience their own annihilation with the annihi-
> lation of our enemies. We must accelerate this process with
> cold ruthlessness, and in doing so we shall be rendering an
> inestimable service to suffering humanity that has been tor-
> tured by Jewry for thousands of years.[11]

In my view, the statements made by Hitler between December
1941 and February 1942 are not the expression of a unique
'basic decision' on the part of the dictator to destroy the
European Jews now that the USA had entered the war. Other
leading representatives of the regime had used similar
formulations before December 1941 to describe the goal of
'annihilating' and 'extirpating' the Jews. But Hitler's statements are evidently an important impetus for radicalising the
whole of 'Jewish policy' after the United States' entry into the
war. To match the radical rhetoric, thoughts of postponing
the 'final solution' to the 'Jewish question' (in the form of a
gigantic deportation programme) until after the end of the
war were now receding, and instead possibilities were being
sought for extending the murders during the war itself.

16

AFTER APPROPRIATE PRIOR APPROVAL BY THE FÜHRER

The Wannsee Conference of 20 January 1942

The Wannsee Conference of 20 January 1942 served Heydrich's intention to present the mass murders in the various occupied areas as part of a general plan – ordered by Hitler and directed by the RSHA – for the 'solution to the European Jewish Question'. This presentation was to take place in the presence of a number of high-ranking functionaries of the Party and the SS, as well as leading ministerial officials, which allowed Heydrich to ensure that they, and especially the ministerial bureaucracy, would share both knowledge of and responsibility for this policy.

The central passage of Heydrich's address concerning the general aims of the future 'Jewish Policy' is as follows:

> After appropriate prior approval by the Führer, emigration as a possible solution has been superseded by a policy of evacuating of the Jews to the East. Although these actions [the deportations that had already been begun] are to be regarded merely as possible alternatives, nonetheless practical experience is already being accumulated in this area that will be of great importance for the impending final solution of the Jewish Question.[1]

First and foremost, therefore, Heydrich was making it clear that the new 'possible solution' had been explicitly authorised by Hitler. On a more detailed level, he was distinguishing precisely between two chronological stages: the 'impending final solution' and the provisional measures intended for the near future, or 'possible interim solutions' (*Ausweich-möglichkeiten*). In the impending 'final solution', according to Heydrich, a total of 11 million Jews would be involved, a figure which was broken down by country in a statistical addendum to the transcript. This list not only includes Jews living in areas under German control, but also those of Great Britain, Ireland, Portugal, Sweden, Switzerland, Spain and Turkey. Included in the 700,000 Jews for unoccupied France are those of the North African colonies. Heydrich thus clearly distinguished the programme of deportations that had already been set into motion from a far more comprehensive plan, whose execution he said was 'dependent on military developments', and could therefore only be realised fully after a German victory. According to the transcript, Heydrich made the following remarks concerning the 'final solution' that he envisaged:

> As part of the development of the final solution, the Jews are now to be put to work in a suitable manner under the appropriate leadership. Organised into large work-gangs and segregated according to sex, those Jews fit for work will be led into these areas as road-builders, in the course of which, no doubt, a large number will be lost by natural wastage.

The remainder who will inevitably survive, who will certainly be those who have the greatest powers of endurance, he adds, will have to be dealt with accordingly in order to prevent their becoming 'the seed-bed of a new Jewish regeneration.' Initially the Jews were to be taken to 'transit-ghettos', from which they were to be 'transported further toward the East'.

Heydrich thus developed the conception of a gigantic deportation programme which would only be fully realisable in the post-war period. The Jews who were to be deported 'to the East' were to be worked to death through forced labour or, if they should survive these tribulations, they would be murdered. The fate of those 'unfit for work', children and mothers in particular, was not further elucidated by Heydrich. In the context of his speech as whole, however, it is clear that these too were to be killed. For as Heydrich said, he wanted to prevent the survival of a 'germ cell of a new Jewish regeneration' at all costs.

Heydrich went on to say that 'in the process of carrying out the final solution', the whole area under German rule would be 'combed through' from West to the East; in the area of Germany, including the Protektorat, these measures would have to have been completed already, by way of 'anticipation'. Here once more the distinction is being made between the 'final solution' realisable only in the long-term, and the smaller, 'anticipatory' steps already underway. Jews over the age of sixty-five, Heydrich goes on to say, should be removed to an old-people's ghetto (*Altersghetto*) in Theresienstadt. This special regulation for the elderly was designed to lend the idea of a labour programme in the East a degree of added plausibility.

Heydrich's exposition indicates that the RSHA was at this time still proceeding according to the plan, followed since the beginning of 1941, of implementing the 'final solution' after the end of the war in the occupied Eastern areas. Heydrich also made clear what was understood by the phrase 'final solution': the Jewish people were to be annihilated through a combination of forced labour and mass murder. The fact that it was Jewish forced labour that gained importance at the turn of 1941/42 speaks in favour of taking Heydrich's remarks literally.[2] On the other hand, there is no evidence to suggest that there were already plans at this point in time to deport the Jews straight out of Central and Western Europe into extermination camps. On the contrary, the first deportations from non-German countries (Slovakia and France) which began in March and April 1942, as well as the simultaneous 'third wave' of deportations from Germany were not to lead directly to the gas chambers of the extermination camps. Neither immediately before nor after the Wannsee Conference, but only in late spring 1942 was the capacity of the extermination camps suddenly and hurriedly expanded.

The transcript of the Wannsee Conference does however make it clear that the idea of a post-war solution was being firmly adhered to, whilst at the same time there was a debate over the proposal to exempt the Jews in the General-gouvernement Poland and the occupied Soviet Areas from this general plan and kill them in the short-term.

Five weeks prior to the Wannsee Conference General-gouverneur Frank had already learned in Berlin that the deportation of the Jews from the Generalgouvernement Poland could not be counted on, even in the medium-to-long-term.[3] As Reichsleiter, Frank was part of the group of people to whom Hitler had announced the impending 'annihilation' of the Jews on 12 December 1941. He drew the consequences of this knowledge at a meeting on 16 December in Cracow:

In Berlin they said to us 'What is all this trouble for? We can't do anything with them in the Ostland or in the Reichskommissariat [Ukraine], liquidate them yourselves!' Gentlemen, I must ask you, arm yourselves against all considerations of compassion. We must annihilate the Jews wherever we come upon them and wherever this is at all possible, in order to preserve intact the [entire] structure of the Reich.[4]

The method and time-frame for this mass murder were still open in mid-December 1941, as we can see from Frank's further remarks:

> These 3.5 million Jews cannot be shot, we cannot poison them, but we will be able to intervene in such a way that will somehow lead to a successful extermination – in the context of the greater measures from the Reich that are to be discussed. The Generalgouvernement Poland must become just as free of Jews [*judenfrei*] as the Reich. Where and how that happens is a matter for the official bodies that we must set up and run, and whose effectiveness I will inform you of in due course.

The determination of the leadership of the Generalgouvernement Poland to achieve this 'successful extermination' in the short-term within the Generalgouvernement Poland itself is the background to the remarks of the representative of the government of the Generalgouvernement Poland, Secretary of State (Staatssekretär) Bühler, near the end of the Wannsee Conference. He stated that the Generalgouvernement Poland would:

> welcome the initiation of the final solution to this question in the Generalgouvernement Poland, because the problem of transportation does not play a decisive role here and because problems related to labour will not obstruct the course of this action.

In addition, the approximately 2.5 million Jews who were to be removed from the Generalgouvernement Poland 'as soon as possible' were overwhelmingly 'unfit to work'. Bühler followed this with a clear proposal to murder the majority of the Jews of the Generalgouvernement Poland in the Generalgouvernement itself.

Then they discussed the question of how the Jews of the Generalgouvernement Poland and the occupied Soviet Areas were actually to be 'removed' – in other words, they talked concretely about the methods for murder:

> In the concluding stages different possible solutions were discussed. Both Gauleiter Dr Meyer [the representative of the Ministry for the occupied Eastern Territories] and Staatssekretär Dr Bühler took the position that certain preliminary measures in the process of the final solution should immediately be put into effect in the relevant area itself, but necessarily in such a way as to avoid causing disquiet amongst the local population.

The transcript does not give any evidence that a decision was taken on the proposals of Meyer and Bühler at the conference itself.

17

IN THIS MATTER THE FÜHRER IS THE UNTIRING PIONEER AND SPOKESMAN FOR A RADICAL SOLUTION

The Extension of the Deportations and Mass Murders in Spring 1942

After the Wannsee Conference, the RSHA continued planning for the deportation of the Jews from Greater Germany and expanded it to an initial European deportation programme, encompassing a total of six countries in the first instance.

In an express letter to the main and subsidiary offices of the Gestapo of 31 January 1942, Eichmann made it clear that 'the recent evacuations of Jews from individual areas to the East' represented 'the beginning of the final solution to the Jewish Question in the Ostmark and in the Protektorat of Bohemia and Moravia.'¹

From a discussion between Eichmann and representatives of the main Gestapo offices on 6 May, it emerges that a further deportation programme for the whole of Germany had been set up within the RSHA, namely what Heydrich had already announced in November 1941 as 'the third wave'² Eichmann explained that in the course of this next programme 55,000 Jews would be deported from the territory of Germany inclusive of the Ostmark and the Protektorat. He also announced that most of the remaining Jews from the Altreich (Germany within the borders of 1937) would in all probability be forcibly removed to Theresienstadt (which was then being cleared), in the course of the summer or the autumn of 1942.

Within the framework of this third wave of deportations, Jewish people from different parts of the territory of the

Altreich and from Vienna, as well as Theresienstadt, would be forcibly carried off between March and June 1942 and brought to a series of ghettos in the district of Lublin (in particular Izbica, Piaska, Zamocs and Trawniki). The inhabitants of these ghettos had been deported to the extermination camp Belzec shortly before. As a rule, the deportation trains from Germany stopped in Lublin, where those men 'fit for work' were separated out in order to be put to work in the forced labour camp at Majdanek.[3] There is conclusive proof of forty-three transports, which each usually carried 1,000 people. However, there are indications of further transports, amounting to a probable sixty trains in all.[4]

The deportation of Central European Jews and the extermination of the Eastern European Jews in spring 1942 followed the same pattern as the first two waves of deportations in autumn 1941 and the winter following. The miserable living conditions in the ghettos in the district of Lublin meant that the great majority of the deportees died within few months of their arrival. Those who survived the conditions of the ghetto were generally deported to extermination camps in the Generalgouvernement Poland.

In March 1942, the deportations were also extended to two countries outside Germany. According to the terms of an agreement with Slovakia, young Jews who were 'fit for work' were deported to Majdanek in the district of Lublin and to Auschwitz. Directly after this programme was introduced, and in response to a request from the Germans, the Slovakian government declared their willingness to deport all Slovakian Jews (close to 90,000 people). The deportation of families began on 11 April. By June, eleven trains had arrived in Auschwitz and a further twenty-eight had gone to ghettos in the district of Lublin, or the camp at Majdanek.[5] In France the military administration had decided in December 1941 to send the first hostage-transport of 1,000 Jewish men to the East. Preparations had been made at the beginning of January 1942, but the convoy was not able to leave because of a lack of transport.

After Eichmann had agreed to the deportation of those 1,000 people on 1 March,[6] a discussion within the RSHA of 4 March resulted in a decision to propose the deportation of a further 'c. 5,000 Jews to the East' to the French government. This was recorded by Theodor Dannecker, the expert on Jewish matters in the Paris Gestapo.[7] Dannecker also told Carltheo Zeitschel, the Embassy staff-member in charge of Jewish affairs, that Heydrich had given an assurance to the effect that, after the deportation of the first 1,000 people, 'a further 5,000 Jews would be transported in the course of 1942' and that he had 'agreed that further, even larger transports could be carried out in 1943'.[8] While the first transport – which left on 27 March 1942 and arrived in Auschwitz on 30 March[9] – was still described as a reprisal against the French resistance, the coming 'hostage-transports' were to be part of a concrete programme of deportations.

The deportation of 5,000 people to Auschwitz that Heydrich had announced at the beginning of March 1942 was carried out between 5 June and 17 July. At this point these five transports, as well as the transports of families from Slovakia that started in April, were already part of the RSHA's first European-wide deportation-programme. An important piece of evidence as to the existence of this programme is found in a note from the office of the Slovakian Prime Minister, Votech Tuka, dated 10 April and concerning a visit by Heydrich.[10] On this occasion Heydrich explained to Tuka that the planned deportation of Slovakian Jews was only 'a part of the programme'. At the time, he said, there was a 'resettlement' of altogether 'half a million' Jews 'out of Europe to the East'. Besides Slovakia, Germany, the Protektorat, the Netherlands, Belgium and France were affected.

On 11 June 1942 a discussion took place in the Department for Jewish affairs in the Reich Security Main Office (*Reichssicherheitshauptamt*). The German experts on Jewish affairs stationed in Paris, The Hague and Brussels gathered to discuss the occupied Western European part of the general European deportation programme. Dannecker, the expert for Jewish affairs of the Gestapo in Paris, made a note to himself stating that Himmler had given the order to 'deliver larger quantities of Jews to the Auschwitz concentration camp, to increase the workforce'. 'This is on the primary condition that the Jews (of both sexes) be between 16 and 40 years old. 10% who are not fit for work can be sent with them.' Starting on 13 July, 15,000 Jews were to be deported from the Netherlands, 10,000 from Belgium and 100,000 from France.[11]

In parallel with the deportations, the mass murders were extended in the 'reception areas' and elsewhere.

Preparations for the 'resettlement' of Jews from the districts of Lublin and Galicia can be traced back to January 1942.[12] By this time 'resettlement' was clearly a euphemism for their planned mass murder. In mid-March the liquidation of the Lublin ghetto marked the beginning of the systematic murder of those Jews 'unfit for work' in the district of Lublin, which had been in planning since the decision to build the extermination camp, Belzec, in autumn 1941.[13] The bloody liquidation of the ghettos and the deportations to Belzec thus started at precisely the time that the deportation trains were arriving in the area of Lublin from Germany and Slovakia. Like the Warthegau the previous year, and like the mass executions in the ghettos of Riga and Minsk in November and December 1941,[14] local Jews were murdered in order to make 'room' for the deported Jews. The presence of Himmler in Lublin on 14 March, two days before the clearing of the ghetto, underscores the interest the Himmler had taken in the 'Jewish Policy' in the district of Lublin from the beginning.[15] At the same time as the mass murder commenced in the district of Lublin in mid-March 1942, the SS began the liquidation of the ghettos and the deportations in the district of Galicia.[16] The escalation of the extermination policy in this district should not be seen in the context of the programme of deportation in Central Europe but in relation to the mass murders in the Soviet Union. Galicia had been occupied by the Soviet Union between 1939 and 1941, and was conquered by the Wehrmacht in 1941; from the summer of 1941, and with increased force in October 1941, German units had carried out mass executions, and by the end of 1941 60,000 people had been killed here.[17]

Some light is cast on the annihilation policy in these two districts by a remark in Goebbels' diary from 27 March 1942, according to which 'a barbaric procedure that I will not describe in more detail is being applied, and of the Jews them-selves there is now not much left.' He says, 'that 60% of them must be liquidated whilst only 40% can be used for work'.[18] In this note Goebbels leaves no doubt about Hitler's respon-sibility for the mass murder:

> A penalty will be exacted from the Jews, and whilst it may be barbaric, they have deserved it. The prophecy that the Führer made for their having caused a new world war is beginning to be realised in the most terrible manner. In these matters we must have no truck with sentimentality. If we did not defend

ourselves from them, the Jews would destroy us. It is a life-and-death struggle between the Aryan race and the Jewish bacillus. No other government and no other regime could summon the strength necessary to solve this question across the board. In this matter, too, the Führer is the untiring pioneer and spokesman for a radical solution that is demanded by the very nature of things and which is therefore inevitable. Thank God the war means that we now have a whole series of possibilities that were denied to us in peacetime. We must exploit these possibilities.

A few days previously Goebbels had reported on a meeting with Hitler:

At the end we spoke about the Jewish question once more. In this matter the Führer is still unrelenting. The Jews must be driven out of Europe, if necessary by using the most brutal of means.[19]

At the same time as the deportations from the districts of Lublin and Galicia were beginning – in mid-March 1942 – in Serbia the SS began the murder of those Jews who had survived the 'retaliatory measures' in the previous autumn. The RSHA informed the Commander of the Security Police in Belgrade of the impending arrival of a gas van. With the aid of this vehicle, by the beginning of May 1942 about 500 men as well as about 7,000 women and children who had been imprisoned in the Belgrade camp of Sajmiste were murdered.[20] This meant that about 90 per cent of all Jews living in Serbia had been killed.

The German procedure in Serbia followed the same model as in the Soviet Union, albeit at a slightly later stage: first the

Jewish men were shot under the pretext of 'retaliation' and in a later phase their dependants were killed, all of them, in accordance with the plan that had been drawn up.

18

THE FÜHRER HAS LAID THE IMPLEMENTATION OF THIS VERY DIFFICULT ORDER ON MY SHOULDERS

The Extension of the Extermination Policy to
the Whole of Europe in Spring and Summer
1942

A further escalation of the extermination policy can be observed in the period between May and June 1942. Previously the mass murders had been restricted to individual regional areas and had been represented as responses to problems arising in these areas by the responsible authorities. Now, from May and June 1942, the extermination policy was extended to the entire area under German control. By the middle of 1942 the authorities had come to understand that the mass murders were no longer regionally limited advances in the direction of the 'final solution' that was to be accomplished in its full scope only after the end of the war, but that an intensification and extension of these murders was now intended to achieve this 'final solution' during the course of the war itself, and that it was to be achieved using the killing machinery originally intended for mass murders in the separate regions.

At the end of May/June 1942, the systematic mass murder of Jews in the districts of Lublin and Galicia was extended to all Districts of the Generalgouvernement Poland. The killing of the great majority of Polish Jews bears all the signs of an operation executed according to a plan. It is significant that HSSPF Friedrich-Wilhelm Krüger was appointed State Secretary for Security in May, and that the order of 3 June that established his new position gave him the mandate to take charge of all 'Jewish Affairs'.[1] In May, the extermination camp Sobibor was opened, while Belzec was closed temporarily from the middle of April until the end of May so that its killing capacity could be extended. In May, or June at the latest, the construction of a third extermination camp, Treblinka, had began in the district of Warsaw.[2] In the district of Lublin, systematic deportations from the local districts began in May, independently of the arrival of transports from Central Europe.[3] These transports were going to Sobibor, where the deportees were murdered. From the end of May, the transports from the district of Cracow to Belzec started.[4] The initiation of deportations from the other districts was delayed by a ban on the use of transportation that was imposed in mid-June because of the imminent summer offensive on the Eastern front. At a meeting dealing with police matters in Cracow, there was general agreement that 'the problem of Jewish resettlement is forcing us to make a decision' as HSSPF Krüger put it. After the ban on the use of transportation had been lifted, the 'action against the Jews' was to be 'implemented with greater intensity'.[5] The deportations from the district of Cracow to Belzec were resumed immediately following the lifting of the ban. At this point, Sobibor was shut down until October because of repairs being carried out to the railway line; in the meantime, larger gas chambers were being installed there.

For the other four districts of the Generalgouvernement Poland the picture is as follows: Between 22 July and 12 September 1942, 250,000 people were deported from the Warsaw Ghetto to Treblinka, where they were murdered. At the end of July the deportations to Belzec from the districts of Lublin and Galicia resumed;[6] at the beginning of August, the deportations from the district of Radom to Treblinka began.[7]

The systematic murder of the Jews in the annexed area of Upper Silesia also began in mid-May. By August, 38,000

people would be deported, 20,000 to the gas chambers of
Auschwitz, the rest to forced labour camps.[8]

In May 1942 a fourth wave of deportations from Germany
was set in motion. The transports to Minsk were resumed:
about 26,000 people were brought to Minsk from the area of
the 'Greater German Reich' in twenty-three transports
between May and September.[9] However, the *modus operandi*
of the exterminations was new. The deportees were no
longer imprisoned in ghettos; instead, the trains went on to a
station near the estate of Maly Trostinez; there almost all of
the deportees were shot on the spot or poisoned in gas vans.[10]
Between August and December the remaining transports in
the fourth wave of deportations from Germany went, almost
without exception, straight into the extermination camps of
Auschwitz and Treblinka.[11]

Similarly, from June onwards the Jews arriving from
Slovakia and the district of Lublin were no longer brought to
ghettos but were deported straight to the extermination
camps of Sobibor.[12]

The new stage in the escalation that began early in 1942
led to the abandonment of the concept of 'transit-ghettos'
for Jews coming from Central Europe. Another consequence
of this further radicalisation was that between 4 and 15 May
the Jews who had been deported to Lodz from Central
Europe in the previous autumn – almost 11,000 people who
had survived the devastating conditions in the ghetto – were
murdered by gas vans stationed in Chelmno.[13]

In May the civil authorities and the SS in the occupied
Soviet zones began a new wave of murders, which ended,
in the summer, with the almost total destruction of the
Jewish civilian population.[14] On 28 July Himmler wrote
to Gottlob Berger, the head of the main SS office, 'the

occupied Eastern zones are being cleansed of Jews. The Führer has laid the implementation of this very difficult order on my shoulders. In any case, no-one can relieve me of the responsibility.'

From mid-July the programme of deportations from Western Europe had been set in motion. These transports went to Auschwitz. The trains from Slovakia had now also been redirected to Auschwitz, as the first of the fourth-wave trains from Germany had been. After the completion of provisional gas chambers in two farm houses (Bunkers I and II), what had been begun during May in Minsk and in June at Sobibor now took place in Auschwitz from 4 July onwards: beginning with the transports from Slovakia, the SS now started to murder the majority of the deportees in the gas chambers immediately after their arrival and after a 'selection process' had taken place on the ramp.[15]

In July 1942, after the transportation ban had been lifted, the Europe-wide programme of deportations and killings had thus come fully into operation. The individual elements of this programme, and their co-ordination within a system designed for complete extermination is manifest. This system may be characterised as follows: definition of Jews, deprivation of their rights, and expropriation; concentration in transition camps and ghettos; deportation; deliberately engineered high mortality rate in the phase of concentration and deportation; selection of those 'fit for work'; murder of those 'unfit' for work or those not needed for work via mass executions or by means of gas; 'extermination through work'; strict secrecy; systematic covering of traces.

Immediately after Himmler had convinced himself during an inspection tour of Auschwitz in July[16] that the extermination programme had begun, he established, on 19 July, a

concrete schedule for the extermination of the Jews of the
Generalgouvernement Poland: by the end of the year, the
Jews of the Generalgouvernement Poland were to be killed,
excepting only a small remaining group of Jews 'fit for work',
who were to be placed under the control of the SS.[17]
Himmler's demand had immediate repercussions on the
deportations in the Generalgouvernement Poland where,
from 22 July onward, 5,000 people a day had been deported
from Warsaw alone to the extermination camp at Treblinka.[18]

The renewed escalation that began in May and June can,
in the main only be reconstructed, on the basis of the events,
the deportations and mass murders in the extermination
camps. The real decision-making process is obscure. One can
certainly identify a link with the general radicalisation of
Jewish policy after the Americans' entry into the war, but it
was months before the impulse that resulted from this radicalisation – which was by no means a 'single decision' – took
the form of concrete measures. It is striking, however, that a
few weeks before the murders were decisively extended (end
of April and the beginning of May 1942), Himmler met
Heydrich seven times in three places within the space of a
week: first in Berlin on 25 April, twice on 26 April (at the
second of these meetings Kurt Daluege, the chief of the Order
Police, was also present), and on 27 April; then in Munich on
28 and 30 April, and on 2 May in Prague for which Himmler
made a special journey. This series of discussions was framed
by two longer meetings between Himmler and Hitler, which
took place on 23 April and 3 May 1942 in the Führer's headquarters.[19] Whether or not the Europe-wide extension of the
murder of the Jews was indeed discussed by Hitler and the
leadership of the SS in a series of meetings at this time is initially only a matter for speculation, and must be examined by

further research. It is quite possible that the escalation of Jewish persecution that began in May gained a further impetus from the assassination attempt on Heydrich (27 May) and his death (4 June), and that this drove those responsible to push their plans ahead more vigorously. The fact that responsibility for the death of one of those most heavily responsible for the persecution of the Jews should first and foremost be laid at the door of 'the Jews' was, in the twisted logic of the National Socialists, perfectly obvious. As a reaction to his death, 1,000 Jews were deported from Prague to Majdanek 'in retaliation',[20] and Himmler made it clear in his speech to the police and SS chiefs on the occasion of Heydrich's funeral in Berlin that the programme of murders was to be completed as soon as possible: 'The migration of the Jewish people will be done with within a year. Then no more of them will be migrating'.[21]

In the period around the second half of April 1942, the previous *modus operandi* for the mass murder of the Jews was altered: up to this point, the Jews of Central Europe had been deported to the Eastern European ghettos, where the local Jewish population labelled 'not fit for work' had been murdered. Now, in the period between April and July, a step-by-step European-wide murder programme was to be set in motion. Those Jews no longer fit to work would be deported directly to the extermination camps, while those who could still work were to be killed by the most strenuous work under the most extreme conditions. This programme included the murder of those who had been previously spared, those Central European Jews already deported to the East.

A direct order by Hitler initiating this entire programme has not been found. It is, however, unthinkable that these last steps in the escalation of 'Jewish policy' of the Third Reich could have taken place without Hitler's express consent. From the beginning of the Russian campaign, Hitler had expressed himself in the most drastic manner imaginable about the 'solution' to the Jewish question, and he would continue to do so until the end of his life.[22]

As has been demonstrated, Hitler had been constantly involved with 'Jewish policy' in its individual phases, he had issued important orders in this area himself and had even occupied himself with details. Over and over again, Hitler had personally radicalised the persecution of the Jews or recommended such radicalisation: he had urged the mass executions of Poles and Jews in 1939-40; he had repeatedly pushed forward the deportation plans in the years 1939 to 1941; his precepts had decisively influenced the ideological campaign against the Soviet Union; he had pushed forward the deportation of the Central-European Jews from 1941 onwards, and by means of various statements after 1941 he had demanded the 'annihilation' of European Jews. Finally, it has been made evident that the extension of the policy of extermination beyond the occupied Soviet areas from autumn 1941 onwards was a complex undertaking that involved not only many SS and police offices but also a whole series of organisations beyond Himmler's sphere of influence – such as the German occupation authorities, the Foreign Ministry, various other ministries of Germany, the huge organisation of the German railway, and many others. Only Hitler had the authority to bring together these various organisations to carry out a complex task.

It was also in this phase, just as in the years between 1933 and 1939, that Hitler repeatedly slowed down the very radicalisation of the anti-Jewish policy that he himself had decisively accelerated, doing so when it came into conflict with other elements of his policy. Thus in the autumn of 1939 he put a stop to the Nisko project, and in the spring of 1941 he stopped further deportations into the Generalgouvernement Poland because they interfered with military campaigns. Himmler's order for the provisional cessation of the mass executions of German Jews, given at the end of November 1941, will have been in accordance with the intentions of Hitler, who at that point was still hesitating about having the Central and West European Jews murdered as well as the East European Jews. However, such measures for restricting the persecutions were always taken against the background of tactical considerations; they were provisional in nature, and must always be seen in the general context of the policy of extermination that was decisively determined by Hitler.

Even in this phase, the terminology used by Hitler and other leading National Socialists still maintained the idea of an 'evacuation' (*Aussiedlung, Evakuierung*) or 'resettlement' (*Umsiedlung*) in the East and a 'territorial final solution' to be found after the end of the war 'outside Europe'. An example is Goebbels' diary entry for 27 April 1942:

I spoke with the Führer once again in great detail about the Jewish question. His point of view on this problem is unrelenting. He wants to drive the Jews out of Europe altogether. And that is the right thing to do. The Jews have brought so much misfortune upon our Continent that the most severe punishment that could be imposed upon them would still be too mild. Himmler is at the moment carrying out a great resettlement of Jews from German cities to the Eastern ghettos.

Hitler expressed himself similarly again on 29 May 1942, according to Goebbels:

> [one must] liquidate the Jewish threat at all costs. [...] Therefore the Führer does not at all want the Jews to be evac-uated to Siberia. There, even under the harshest conditions they would still undoubtedly represent a vital force. He would rather resettle them in Central Africa. There they would live in a climate that would certainly not make them strong and resistant. In any case, it is the Führer's aim to make the whole of Western Europe free of Jews.[23]

As we have already seen, Goebbels had known of the mass murders in the Generalgouvernement Poland since March 1942, and had described Hitler as the originator of this policy.[24] That both he and Hitler apparently still clung to the idea of a 'resettlement' of the Jews in April and May of that year can be attributed either to the consistent use of 'camou-flaging' terminology,[25] or to the fact that even those who were responsible for the mass murders up to this point persisted in the view that the real 'final solution' would take place at a later point and that it would only be adopted in full after the end of the war, so that the murders so far were only 'provisional' measures, or 'anticipations' of the 'final solution'.[26] Only in spring and early summer 1942 was it grad-ually realised that the 'final solution' was to be implemented during the course of the war itself.

The statements about possible 'resettlement projects' that Hitler made after this point, that is from the summer of 1942, are thus unquestionably diversions meant to deceive his lis-teners. This is true, for example, of his remarks during the evening of 24 July 1942, when Goebbels tried to make his guests believe that the Führer had nothing to do with the murder of the Jews that was being rumoured.

> After the end of the war, he will rigorously adopt the stance that says he will smash to pieces city after city if the filthy Jews don't come out and emigrate to Madagascar or some other Jewish national state [...] When it was reported to him that Lithuania was also free of Jews, that was therefore significant.[27]

At this point the Foreign Ministry had already closed its files on Madagascar five months earlier. This had been done in February, referring explicitly to a decision taken by Hitler.[28]

19

IN ACCORDANCE WITH THE WISHES OF THE FÜHRER

Further Extension of the Extermination Policy from Summer 1942

We have numerous further statements by Hitler from the period 1942-45 that show how he intervened continually in 'anti-Jewish policy' and tried to impel it forwards as a more radical 'solution'.

When the extermination policy was extended to the whole of Europe in spring and summer 1942, one group was initially excluded from the campaign of murders: young Jews between sixteen and thirty-two, capable of being set to work. This was a concession first made by Himmler in the face of incontestable demands placed by those responsible for forced labour, but in the coming months he and other radical National Socialists attempted to put an end to it. The progress of these attempts shows that the only possible way of reversing this concession was via Hitler himself.

One of the rabble-rousers was the Minister for Propaganda and Gauleiter of Berlin, Goebbels. From Goebbels' diary entry of 29 May 1942 it emerges that on Goebbels' insistence, Hitler agreed to instruct Albert Speer to 'make sure as soon as possible that Jews presently working in the German armaments industry be replaced by foreign workers'.[1] In September 1942 once more, speaking at an armaments conference, Hitler was to insist that 'removing Jews from armament works in the Reich' was an important priority.[2] A few days later, Hitler 'once more expressed [to Goebbels] his firm intention of bringing the Jews out of Berlin come what may', according to Goebbels' diaries. In so far as this group of people were at all active in production, it would not be difficult to replace them with for-eign workers.[3] On the following day, in a speech at the Berlin Sportpalast, Hitler reminded his audience once more of his prophecy of 30 January 1939, and again threatened to 'exter-minate' the European Jews.[4]

At the armament conference in September 1942, men-tioned above, Hitler had expressed agreement with a proposal from Fritz Sauckel (his special commissioner for forced labour) to continue using qualified Jewish skilled workers in the Generalgouvernement Poland as a temporary measure in view of the appalling shortage of workers.[5]

Then on 9 October 1942 Himmler gave the order that 'so-called armament workers' in textile firms and the like in Warsaw and Lublin should be collected in concentration camps. The Jews in the 'real armament industries' were to be progressively released from these factories, so that eventually there would only be 'a very few Jewish large-scale concen-tration camp enterprises [Kl-Großbetriebe, where Kl = Konzentrationslager, concentration camps] in the East of the Generalgouvernement Poland if at all possible'. 'Nevertheless, the Jews will also have to disappear from there as well, in accordance with the wishes of the Führer.'[6]

The shifting of the Jewish workforce from ghettos to the concentration camps did not only worsen their living condi-tions, it also had a diabolical consequence that is not evident at first reading of the document. In the ghettos, the families of the Jewish workforce were also kept alive, but in the con-centration camps, where families were split up, this was not the case. Jewish mothers and their children in particular were usually murdered in the gas chambers immediately after their arrival. Himmler's order to restrict the use of Jewish labour in the Generalgouvernement Poland only to the concentration camps therefore meant the death sentence for their families and dependants.

Furthermore it can be documented that Hitler kept himself informed about the progress of the systematic murder of the Jews living in occupied Soviet territory. On 29 December 1942, Himmler presented Hitler with the 'Report to the Führer on Combating Gangs and Mobs', no. 51. This was specially prepared in large 'Führer-type' (so that Hitler could read it without his glasses) and his adjutant's manuscript note at the top of its first page records that it was submitted to him on 31 December. This report[7] covered the period from August to November 1942, and referred only to parts of the occupied Soviet area (southern Russia, Ukraine and the district of Bialystok); it included the following statistics concerning persons imprisoned or executed:

1 Bandits
  a) established number of deaths after combat, 1,337
  b) prisoners executed immediately, 737
  c) prisoners executed after lengthy thorough
     interrogation, 7,828

2 Gang helpers and suspects
  a) arrested, 16,553
  b) executed, 14,257
  c) Jews executed, 363,211

According to this, of 387,370 people killed altogether, more than 90 per cent were Jews. This document shows that, in accordance with Hitler's orders to Himmler of 18 December 1942, Jews were indeed exterminated as 'Partisans', systematically and on a large scale.

Immediately after the start of the deportation programme from Western and Central European countries in summer 1942, the Germans continued to make efforts to include other states in the extermination programme.

As early as July, the decision was taken to approach the Croation government with the demand that they hand over their Jews to the Germans. This step led to the deportation in August of about 5,000 Croatian Jews to Auschwitz, where they were murdered.[8]

In July 1942, Finland – a German ally – seems also to have attracted the attention of the SS. According to a report by the Finnish Prime Minister, Johann-Wilhelm Rangell, submitted after the war, Himmler is said to have used a visit to Finland in July 1942 to raise the subject of 'Finnish Jews'. Rangell said he cut the discussion short and it was not raised again on the German side thereafter.[9]

Also in July, Gustav Richter, the German advisor on 'Jewish questions' in the Bucharest embassy, and the Deputy Minister President Mihai Antonescu agreed that the deportation of the Rumanian Jews that had already been authorised by Marshal Antonescu should begin on 10 September.[10]

However, this agreement led to an intervention by Ribbentrop, the Foreign Minister. Ribbentrop felt that he had been bypassed by this agreement and instructed the German Section of the Foreign Ministry, which was closely allied to the SS leadership, to continue with the measures agreed with Rumania but not to develop any further initiatives with respect to Hungary, Bulgaria and the Italian-occupied zones in Croatia.[11]

With respect to Hungary, this instruction only represented a confirmation of the policy adopted by the German Section of the Foreign Ministry and the RHSA in summer 1942. At

this point, both sides were in agreement that anti-Jewish legislation was not yet far enough advanced in Hungary and that
therefore the prerequisites for a comprehensive deportation
plan were not in place.[12]

For the same reason the German side had so far shown
itself to be uninterested in deportations from Bulgaria. Only
after the Bulgarian government had intensified its anti-Jewish
legislation during the summer, quite clearly under the influence of the events in Croatia and Rumania, did the RSHA
begin to put pressure on the Foreign Ministry in September
to approach Bulgaria about beginning deportations.[13]

Similarly, during the summer the Foreign Ministry
approached the Italian government with a demand that they
should hand over the Jews living in the Italian areas of occupation in Croatia. This peremptory request was at first treated
positively by Mussolini.[14]

In July 1942 the RHSA had already shown itself to be
interested in an intensification of anti-Jewish measures in
Greece. However, the German side did not succeed in per-
suading the Italians to take parallel measures in their zones of
occupation.[15]

These efforts to extend the deportation programmes were
given renewed impetus at the end of September. On 24
September Ribbentrop gave Luther, the head of his German
Department, the instruction 'to accelerate the evacuation of
the Jews from the various countries in Europe as fast as possible.' The Bulgarian, Hungarian and Danish governments
were to be approached; he would himself take care of further
steps to be taken in the case of Italy.[16] This instruction indicates a sudden about-turn in the policy of the Foreign
Ministry. On 25 August, Ribbentrop had still been declaring
himself against taking the initiative in the 'Jewish question' in

respect of Hungary, Bulgaria and the Italian-occupied zones in Croatia.[17] This shift on the part of Ribbentrop probably took place in response to a decision of Hitler, who had obviously decided to step up the 'Jewish policy'. Hitler and Ribbentrop had discussed the 'Jewish problem' with the Croatian Premier, Ante Pavelic, on 24 September (the day on which Ribbentrop issued his new instruction).[18] The day before, 23 September, both had received the Rumanian Deputy Minister President, Mihai Antonescu, and Antonescu had used this opportunity once more to underline his intention of deporting the Rumanian Jews.[19] Immediately before this, at the armament conference held between 20 and 22 September, Hitler had declared himself in favour of deporting the Jews still occupied in the armament industry in Germany, and at the end of the month he talked again in massively anti-Semitic terms.[20]

In fact, in the last months of 1942 almost all the allies that had become involved in the German deportation plans were to distance themselves from them once more. In Slovakia deportations were completely halted by October 1942; Rumania postponed the agreement to begin deportations that it had already given, and the Bulgarian and Hungarian governments showed no interest in acceding to German intentions in this matter.[21] Attempts to persuade the Italian government to hand over the Jews living in their zones of occupation ended negatively, despite Mussolini's agreement in September.[22] Finally, the deportation of Jews from Denmark soon proved not to be advantageous from the German perspective. After Denmark had been put on the deportation list in September 1942, probably mainly because of Hitler's extraordinary irritation about the development of the political situation there, the newly appointed Representative of the

Reich, SS-General Werner Best, immediately adopted an elastic occupation policy that was not compatible with an action against the Danish Jews.[23]

Ultimately the only country that was caught up in the deportation machinery of autumn 1942 was Norway. The hurried deportation of more than 500 Norwegian Jews (most of the Jews in Norway were able to escape to Sweden) suggests that a short-term 'substitute solution' had been sought there for the deportations from Denmark that had not taken place.[24]

20

TO BE TREATED LIKE
TUBERCULOSIS BACILLI

Intensification of the Extermination Policy
after the Turning-point in the War, 1942/1943

The extermination policy received a further impetus in German-occupied Europe at the end of 1942 and the beginning of 1943. After the landing of Anglo-American armed forces in North Africa in November 1942, the Allies began to open up a second front in the southern part of mainland Europe, and the German defeat in Stalingrad in January 1943 made it evident that a turning-point had been reached.

Although the possibility of military defeat was no longer to be dismissed out of hand, the National Socialist regime actually intensified the systematic programme of murdering the European Jews. Just as before, irreplaceable, sometimes highly qualified sections of the workforce were worked to death in the space of a few weeks or months, and important personnel and material resources continued to be deployed so as to sustain the deportation machinery and the broad network of camps.

This strikingly irrational attitude cannot be explained simply with reference to anti-Semitic hatred and ideological blindness in the National Socialist leadership. One must also take into account the fact that once German 'Jewish policy' had already cost millions of human lives, so that it now came to occupy a position of decisive importance in the conduct of the war. National Socialist Germany had begun waging a racist war of extermination; the 'removal' (*Beseitigung*) of the Jews of Europe was one of the central aims of this war. It was no longer possible to revise this aim after the murder of so many millions; the National Socialist regime had long since burnt its bridges. In addition, from the regime's perspective the increasing Jewish resistance to German extermination policy – manifested, for example, in the Warsaw ghetto – acted as a confirmation of the National Socialist world-view, according to which they were engaged in fighting a war against the Jews.

Furthermore, the policy of deportations to concentration camps fulfilled an important function within the Germans' policies for alliances and occupation. We have already seen how in the course of 1942 the question of deporting Jews became a significant object for negotiations between Germany and its allies or, in the case of the occupied areas, how it became a significant factor in their occupation policy. 'Jewish policy' was a main agenda item alongside policies on nutrition, armament and labour. Anti-Jewish policy had become an important pin holding together the bloc led by Germany; in the eyes of the regime, a readiness to play into Germany's hands in this matter was a benchmark for the loyalty of its allies and the forces collaborating with Germany in the occupied areas. In the context of a war conducted with the aim of racial extermination, the decision-makers regarded further intensifying the persecution of the Jews as a logical extension of their policies.

At the end of 1942 and the beginning of 1943 an intensification of the persecution of Jews can be detected in various areas under German domination. In the Generalgouvernement Poland, the SS and the civilian authorities had already taken the decisive steps to replace the Jewish workforce that was still in place with non-Jews by the end of 1942. At the beginning of 1943 they began liquidating the fifty-four 'Jewish residential districts' that still existed in the Generalgouvernement Poland. This initially affected primarily the districts of Galicia, Radom and Warsaw.[1] On the occasion of a visit to Warsaw in January 1943, Himmler gave orders for the ghetto there to be destroyed. In March, the Cracow ghetto was liquidated.[2]

Hitler's decision in September 1942 to deport the Jews still occupied in Germany in the production of armaments,[3] was put into practice on 27 January 1943 in an 'action' across the whole of Germany, since the recruitment of 'foreign workers' that had taken place in the meantime had by then produced the necessary replacements. In Berlin alone 7,000 Jews were arrested in the course of the so-called 'factory action'; some of them were taken at their places of work.[4]

Also at the beginning of 1943 plans were begun for deportations from the German-occupied zone in Greece. Between March and May, a total of about 45,000 people from Saloniki, the largest Jewish community, were deported to Auschwitz and murdered there.[5] A repeated attempt to convince the Italians to extend the deportations to their own occupied zone was again unsuccessful. In February 1943 the German side agreed the deportation of 20,000 Jews with the Bulgarian Judenkommissar Aleksandrev Belev. In March more than 11,000 Jews were deported to Treblinka from the areas of Yugoslavia and Greece occupied by the Bulgarians; but in the face of growing protests, deportations from Old Bulgaria were never to be put into practice.[6]

However, the intensification of Jewish persecution most affected France and her North African colonies – a direct response to the allied landings in Morocco and Algeria in November 1942. When German troops then occupied Tunisia, the 85,000 Jews living there also became entangled in the net of German 'Jewish policy': discriminatory special regulations and forced labour were introduced, and about twenty Jewish activists were deported and murdered.[7]

After the whole of France was occupied in November 1942, the Germans made a renewed attempt to include all the Jews living there in the programme of murders, especially those with French citizenship. The decisive order was once more given by Hitler.

For a report to be delivered to Hitler on 10 December 1942, Himmler made a handwritten list of the points which he wanted to raise. Under 'II: SD and Police Affairs' Himmler noted under point 4 the following key words:

Jews in France
600–700,000
other enemies.

Next to these key words can be found a tick and in Himmler's own handwriting the word 'abolish' (*abschaffen*): Himmler had thus raised these points with Hitler and received permission from him to 'abolish', that is to liquidate, the estimated 600,000 to 700,000 Jews in France as well as 'other enemies'.[8]

After the meeting, Himmler sent a note to Müller, head of the Gestapo, in which he stated:

The Führer gave orders that the Jews and other enemies in France should be arrested and deported. This should take place, however, only once he has spoken with [Pierre] Laval [the French Prime Minister] about it. It is a matter of 6–700,000 Jews.[9]

As a direct consequence of this decision by Hitler, the German occupying force organised raids across the whole of France from the beginning of 1943 onwards. In February the deportations began again, and Eichmann made a short visit to Paris during which he presented a full-scale programme for the deportation of all French Jews. For various reasons, particularly because of the resistance of the Italians in their occupation zone in Southern France, this proved impossible to put into action.[10]

At the meeting on 10 December 1942 Himmler presented Hitler with a proposal to set up a work-camp for Jewish hostages from France, Hungary and Rumania, people who had 'influential relatives in the United States', 10,000 people in all. According to a handwritten note by Himmler from the same day, Hitler accepted this proposal. After this meeting, Himmler sent an order to the Head of the Gestapo, Müller, to collect these 10,000 people in a 'special camp'. He noted, 'certainly they should work there, but under conditions whereby they remain healthy and alive.'[11] This order sent to Müller and Himmler's handwritten note about his meeting with Hitler, confirm that it was Hitler's will that those French Jews who were not covered by this exception were not 'to be kept alive' but were to be 'abolished', i.e. to be liquidated.

Also on 10 December, immediately after he had spoken to Hitler about the establishment of the camp for 10,000 Jewish hostages, Himmler asked the dictator about the question of whether they could free Jews in exchange for foreign currency. As part of his preparation for this discussion, Himmler noted 'am not in favour' and 'important ones as hostages'. After the conversation with Hitler he ticked off this point and noted under the word 'currency' Hitler's gloss, 'from outside'.[12] Hitler had therefore not followed Himmler's advice and had agreed that Jews could be exchanged for foreign currency that had to be raised outside the area under German control, as long as this group of people was not more valuable as hostages. The fact that such an exemption had to be specifically authorised by Hitler is further evidence for his control over the whole extermination process.

A further impetus towards the radicalisation of the German policy of extermination can be detected after the beginning of the Warsaw ghetto uprising (19 April–16 May 1943). The National Socialist leadership was in agreement about the need to murder the Jews of the Generalgouvernement Poland in particular as quickly as possible, as Goebbels and Himmler unanimously stressed at the end of April and at the beginning of May.[13] Friedrich-Wilhelm Krüger, Higher SS and Police Leader in the Generalgouvernement Poland, also received an order from Himmler in May, instructing him 'to carry out the removal of the Jews [Entjudung] as quickly as possible' and to cease taking account of Jewish members of the workforce.[14] From the end of April the ghetto liquidations in the district of Lublin that had been begun in March were intensified, whilst between the end of May and the end of June all the ghettos remaining in the district of Galicia were dissolved: this effectively meant the murder of the large majority of the inhabitants. On 23 May 1943 Himmler gave the order for all the Jews in the area of Germany to be deported 'to the East' or to Theresienstadt. This order also specifically mentioned the Jews of Upper Silesia, who were carried off to Auschwitz and forced labour camps between June and August 1943.[15] On 8 June Himmler insisted that the French government be impelled to take away French nationality from the Jews, who had been citizens of France since 1927, and to deport this group into Germany by 15 July. At the same time, Alois Brunner, the RSHA deportation specialist, arrived in Paris with a special unit in order to speed up the deportations.[16] The deportations from the Netherlands were suddenly increased in May 1943 on the orders of the RSHA,[17] and in Croatia, too, where the first wave of deportations had taken place in August 1942, the deportations to Auschwitz were resumed in May 1943.[18] At around the same time the Foreign Ministry attempted to induce Slovakia to resume deportations.[19] In mid-June, Himmler once more had his policy of intensified murder confirmed by the highest authority: after a presentation to Hitler on 19 July 1943, he noted Hitler's decision 'that despite the unrest growing over the next three to four months, the evacuation of the Jews had to be carried out in a radical manner and had to be seen through'.[20]

Italy's departure from the Axis triggered further radicalisation in the persecution of the Jews. Not only were the Jews living in Northern Italy now exposed to German attack, but all those who had so far been living under the protection of the Italian occupation authorities in Croatia, Greece and Southern France were similarly at risk.

At the same time as extending the persecution of Jews to these areas, the German leadership resolved on deporting the Danish Jews. However, Werner Best, Germany's representative in Denmark, allowed the information on the imminent wave of deportations to filter through to the population and did not undertake serious measures against the resulting exodus of Jews from Denmark to Sweden, since at this point a further worsening of relations with the Danish population seemed to him to be counter-productive.[21]

Finally, by the end of the war two more countries were sucked into the mire of the German persecution of the Jews – Hungary and Slovakia. The National Socialist regime had repeatedly exerted pressure on both countries since 1942 to set up or resume deportations. But this aim could only be achieved after German troops had occupied the two countries.

In the case of Hungary there is documentary proof of Hitler's personal interest in the destruction of the Jewish population. At the so-called First Kleßheim Conference of 17 and 18 April 1943, the Hungarian Regent, Admiral Nikolaus Horthy posed the question as to 'what he should do with the Jews' ('since he could hardly kill them'). Ribbentrop, in Hitler's presence, replied in quite unambiguous terms: they were to be 'either destroyed or taken to concentration camps'. Thereupon Hitler remarked in respect of the Polish Jews:

> If the Jews there don't want to work they will be shot. If they can't work, they must rot. They are to be treated like tuberculosis bacilli that might attack healthy bodies. That is not cruel, if one keeps in mind that even innocent natural creatures like hares and deer have to be killed to stop them causing damage.[22]

Almost a year later, after the occupation of Hungary in March 1944, a task force sent to Budapest under Eichmann's command organised the deportations that began on 15 May 1944 and lasted until the beginning of July, when they were stopped by the Hungarians. By that time a total of 433,000 people had been deported to Auschwitz, where most of them were murdered. Eichmann succeeded in carrying out a few individual transports on his own authority after the end of the main wave of deportations; in addition, in October and November 1944, he had tens of thousands of Hungarian Jews driven to the Austrian border on foot in forced marches.[23]

And finally Slovakia: after the German occupation of Slovakia in August 1944 the Germans once again started up the deportations that had been stopped in October 1942. Between September 1944 and March 1945 more than 12,000 Jews were taken away to concentration and extermination camps.

Hitler, therefore, vigorously pursued a further intensification in the persecution of the Jews during the second half of the war. However, it turned out that putting the deportations into practice depended decisively on the willingness shown both by the governments in the occupied countries and by the local administration and police forces to continue to support German anti-Jewish policy in the face of possible defeat. The Germans only succeeded in initiating large-scale deportations in three countries – Northern Italy, Hungary and Slovakia – and they did so only because they established terrorist regimes there that were entirely dependent on the Germans.[24]

21

BY REMOVING THE JEWS

Hitler's Responsibility

A s has been shown in the previous chapters, it can be proved that Hitler also played a leading role in 'Anti-Jewish policy' in the last years of the Third Reich, in the phase of the Final Solution.

Hitler's responsibility for the murder of the European Jews can be seen directly as well as indirectly: on the basis of the way in which the apparatus of power was structured one can assume with complete certainty that an operation like the murder of millions of people in all areas of Europe, an operation therefore with such wide ramifications and necessitating such huge resources in terms of personnel and materials, was only possible with the consent of the man at the top, the man in whom all the various threads came together.

However, Hitler's responsibility for the Holocaust is also susceptible to documentary proof. Initially this includes his attitudes to certain key groups amongst the servants of the regime – his repeated speeches to generals, for example, and other significant instructions for the preparation of the racist campaign of destruction against the Soviet Union in spring 1941, his statements concerning the 'new order' of the occupied Soviet area on 16 July 1941, or his speech to the Reichs and Gauleiter on 12 December 1941.

These utterances were not so much concrete instructions telling others how to act, but were intended to create a particular climate in which the executive organs of the state were made certain that all further forms of radicalisation of the 'Anti-Jewish policy' had the authorisation of the highest representative of the regime. This is true of Hitler's repeated radically anti-Semitic statements to Goebbels or to his dinner guests, and also of his public speeches, in which he returned again and again to his 'prophecy' that he would 'destroy the Jews of Europe' in the event of a world war.

In addition, however, Hitler issued instructions orally, in private conversations, which served to set in motion individual operations as part of the systematic mass murder of the Jews. These consisted of giving individuals authorisation, allowing his subordinates to decide on how the operations were to be executed and significantly they are only preserved in the notes made by those to whom he was talking. The model for such authorisations was the pogrom of 9 November 1938, when Hitler initially gave Goebbels oral instructions, then absented himself, left Goebbels responsible for the further conduct of the pogrom and then re-involved himself during the course of the night (via the Führer's Deputy, amongst other means). There was a similar course of action when Himmler gave Hitler the early plans for the deportation of the Jews to Africa in May 1940. He approved the suggestions in principle and encouraged Himmler to show his plans to Frank.

Hitler gave decisive authorisation for the policy of deporting the European Jews. At the end of 1940 he instructed Heydrich to present a 'project for the Final Solution', which he did in January 1941, and which envisaged the deportation of all the Jews into an area yet to be fixed upon. By the end of May at the latest it had been decided that this would be the Soviet Union, which would have to be conquered. Furthermore, he made a series of individual decisions about plans for deportation. In the middle of September 1941 Hitler ordered the deportation of the Jews from Germany threatening them with 'reprisals' in the event that the USA entered the war. A little later, Heydrich noted his instruction to the effect that the Jews would have to leave 'the whole of Europe'.

On 18 December 1941 Hitler confirmed to Himmler that the Jews were to be 'extirpated as partisans', most probably referring to the occupied Eastern areas. In July 1942 Himmler reported that he had received an instruction from Hitler to render the occupied Eastern areas 'free of Jews'. But Hitler did not let things rest with instructions of such a general kind. It can be proved that in 1941 and 1942 he had the RSHA and Himmler keep him informed about the mass murders in the East.

Furthermore, in September 1942 Hitler ordered the deportation of the Jews still living in Germany, and at the same time he seems to have given the decisive impetus for accelerating the deportations from allied nations. On 10 December 1942 he instructed Himmler to 'get rid of' 600,000–700,000 Jews and other enemies in France. The plan, adumbrated on the same day, to exchange Jews for hard currency as an exception to the policy of mass destruction, also needed the explicit agreement of Hitler. Hitler's instruction in June 1943 to Himmler – for the 'radical implementation' of the plan to 'evacuate' the Jews still alive within three to four months – completes the picture.

Such direct instructions by Hitler have survived in an accidental and fragmentary manner; we are dealing with the remains of what must be a much bigger mass of instructions. Such fragments make it clear that the murder of the European Jews was not the outcome of a single order but the result of a policy pursued by the regime over a relatively long period

of time, which was time and time again driven forward decisively by Hitler himself.

There is in addition a series of unambiguous statements by
Himmler and Hitler from the years 1943 and 1944 on the
question of responsibility for the murder of the Jews. In various addresses during this period Himmler expressed himself
very clearly about the murder of the European Jews by his
SS, and at the same time he referred to having received a
commission for these mass murders. Even if he did not name
one particular name, his listeners knew perfectly well who it
was who had given him this commission, since as
Reichsführer of the SS he was subordinate to one person, and
one person alone, Adolf Hitler.

Addressing a meeting of Gauleiter and Reichsleiter (the
top brass of the Nazi Party) in Posen, Himmler said on 6
October 1943:

> I ask of you only to listen to what I say to you in this gath-
> ering and never to speak of it. We were faced with the
> question: what about the women and children? I decided to
> find a very clear solution to this problem, too. I did not feel
> myself justified in exterminating the men – that is to say,
> therefore, killing them or having them killed – and then allow-
> ing the avenger, in the form of their children, to grow up to
> confront our sons and grandsons. The difficult decision had to
> be taken to make this people disappear from the face of the
> earth. For the organisation that had to carry out this task, it
> was the most difficult that we had ever had.[1]

It is true that Himmler in this speech gives the impression
that the murder of women and children was in large part his
responsibility and undertaken on his initiative ('I decided…');

yet he refers at the end of the paragraph to the most difficult 'task' that 'we had ever had', and not, say, to a task that he had assigned to the SS. In a speech on 5 May 1944 to generals of the Wehrmacht in Sonthofen, Himmler became even clearer:

> The Jewish question has been solved within Germany itself and in general within the countries occupied by Germany. It was solved in an uncompromising fashion appropriate to the life-and-death struggle of our nation for the continued existence of our blood. [...] You can perhaps understand how difficult it was for me to carry out this order that I had been given as a soldier, and which I implemented out of a sense of obedience and absolute conviction. If you say: 'we can understand as far as the men are concerned, but not when it comes to the children', then I must remind you of what I said at the beginning of my address. In this confrontation with Asia we must get used to condemning to oblivion those rules and customs of past European wars to which we have become accustomed and which are more suited to us. In my view, however deeply we may feel in our hearts, we as Germans are not entitled to allow a generation of hate-filled avengers to grow up, whom our children and grandchildren will have to deal with because we were too weak and cowardly and left it to them.[2]

A few weeks later, on 24 May 1944, and again in Sonthofen, he spoke once more to a group of Generals of the Wehrmacht:

> Another question that was decisive for the inner security of the Reich and of Europe, was the Jewish question. It was uncompromisingly solved, according to our orders and according to rational understanding. I believe, Gentleman,

that you know me well enough to know that I am not a bloodthirsty person and not a man to take pleasure or joy in something firm that has to be done. However on the other hand, I have such good nerves and such a developed sense of duty – I can say that much for myself – that, when I recognise something to be necessary, I can carry it through without compromise. I have not considered myself entitled – this concerns specifically the Jewish women and children – to allow the children to grow into the avengers who will then murder our fathers [sic] and our grandchildren. That I would have thought of as cowardly. Consequently the question was uncompromisingly resolved.[3]

In the context of the murder of the Jews, Himmler is thus speaking here unmistakably of an 'order' and of a 'sense of duty'. His way of formulating it – that he considered himself 'entitled' to have the women and children killed as well – speaks for the view that this mass murder was carried out on his own initiative; it also shows, however, that Himmler was firmly convinced that this decision was covered by Hitler's authority and was in accordance with his will.

Himmler expressed himself yet more clearly a few weeks later, on 21 July 1944, once again in the context of ideological-political training for the generals:

It was the most terrible task and the most terrible assignment that an organisation can possibly receive: the task of solving the Jewish question. I may say this once again quite openly in this gathering, in a few words. It is good that we had sufficient firmness to extirpate the Jews in our area.[4]

Hitler himself stated in a speech addressing high officers of
the Wehrmacht on 26 May 1944:

> By removing the Jew, I abolished the possibility of building
> up a revolutionary core or nucleus in Germany. Of course
> one might say to me, 'Yes, couldn't you have solved this more
> simply – or not simply, since all other means would have been
> more complicated – but more humanely?' Gentlemen, fellow
> Officers, we are engaged in a life-and-death struggle. If our
> opponents triumphed in this struggle, then the German
> people would be extirpated.

Hitler describes in the following sentences what sort of grue-
some extirpation would take place, and then goes on to say:

> Here, as well as in general, humanity would entail the worst
> cruelty against one's own people. If I draw the hatred of the
> Jews upon myself, then I would at least like not to miss out
> on the advantages of such hatred. The advantages consist in
> our having a clean, organised body of the Volk, where no
> others can ever again meddle in our affairs.[5]

In his will and testament of 29 April 1945, and thus in what
were literally his last written words, Hitler once more gave
expression to his deep anti-Semitic hatred:

> But I have also never left room for any doubt about the fact
> that if the peoples of Europe are once again to be regarded
> only as parcels of shares held by these international monetary
> and financial conspirators, then that race which is truly the
> guilty party in this murderous struggle will also be called to
> face its responsibility: Jewry! I have also left no-one in the

dark about the fact that, this time, millions of the children of European Aryan peoples will not be allowed to die of hunger, millions of grown men will not be allowed to suffer death, and hundreds of thousands of women and children will not be allowed to be burnt and bombed to death in the cities without the true culprit being made to pay for his crime, even though it may be by more humane methods. [...]

Above all I pledge the leadership of the nation and its followers to the scrupulous observance of the racial laws and to implacable opposition to the universal poisoner of all peoples, international Jewry[6]

LIST OF ABBREVIATIONS

AA	Auswärtiges Amt	ed.	editor
Abt.	Abteilung	eingel.	eingeleitet
ADAP	Akten zur Deutschen	EG	Einsatzgruppe
	Auswärtigen Politik	EK	Einsatzkommando
AOK	Armee-	EM	Ereignismeldung
	Oberkommando		UdSSR
AGK	Archivum Glowwna	Gestapo	Geheime
	Komisja Badania		Staatspolizei
	Zbrodni Hitlerowskich	GFP	Geheime
	w Polsce		Feldpolizei
APL	Archivum Panstwowe	GG	Generalgouvernement
	w Lublinie	GStA	Geheimes Staatsarchiv
BAB	Bundesarchiv Berlin	Hg.	Herausgeber
BAM	Bundesarchiv/	HGS	Holocaust and
	Militärchiv (Freiburg)		Genocide Studies
Batl.	Bataillon	HSSPF	Höherer SS- und
BDC	Berlin Document		Polizeiführer
	Center	IMT	International
Bd.	Band		Military Tribunal
BdS	Befehlshaber der	IfZ	Institut für
	Sicherheitspolizei		Zeitgeschichte
Biuletyn	Biuletyn Glownej	KTB	Kriegstagebuch
	Komisji Badania	KZ	Konzentrationslager
	Zbrodni	LG	Landgericht
	Hitlerowskich w	MBliV	Ministerialblatt für
	Polsce		die innere Verwaltung
CDJC	Centre de	NA	National Archives
	Documentation Juive		(Washington)
	Contemporaine (Paris)	NS, ns	Nationalsozialismus,
CdZ	Chef der		nationalsozialistisch
	Zivilverwaltung	NSDAP	Nationalsozialistische
DiM	Dokumenty i		Deutsche
	Materialy		Arbeiterpartei

OKW	Oberkommando der Wehrmacht	VB	Völkischer Beobachter
OS	Osobi-Archiv (Moskau)	VfZ	Vierteljahrshefte für Zeitgeschichte
PAA	Politisches Archiv des Auswärtigen Amtes (Bonn)	VO	Verordnung
		VOGG	Verordnungslblatt für das Generalgouvernement
RFSS	Reichsführer SS	vol.	volume
RGBl	Reichsgesetzblatt	WL	Wiener Library (London)
RMBliV	Reichsminiterialblatt für die innere Verwaltung	WLB	Wiener Library Bulletin
RSHA	Reichssicherheitshauptamt	YIVO	Yidischer Visenschaftlikher Institut (New York)
SD	Sicherheitsdienst		
Sipo	Sicherheitspolizei	YV	Yad Vashem (Jerusalem)
SK	Sonderkommando	z.b.V.	zur besonderen Verwendung
SS	Schutzstaffel		
StA	Staatsarchiv	ZSt	Zentrale Stelle der Landesjustizverwaltungen zur Aufklärung nationalsozialisticher Verbrechen (Ludwigsburg)
STA	Staatsanwaltschaft		
SUA	Státny Ústredni Archiv (Prague)		
SWCA	Simon Wiesenthal Center Annual		
USHM	United States Holocaust Museum (Washington)	ZUV	Zentraler Untersuchungsvorgang

NOTES

PREFACE

1 Lipstadt, *Denying.*
2 For an introduction to this material, see Longerich, *Holocaust.*
3 Krausnick/Wilhelm, *Einsatzgruppen*; Hildebrand, *Third Reich*; Burrin, *Hitler.*
4 Fleming, *Hitler.*
5 Browning, *Months*, idem, *Weg,* and idem, *Nazi Policy*; Broszat, *Hitler.*
6 Kershaw, *Hitler.*
7 Longerich, *Politik.*

CHAPTER 1

1 Kershaw, *Hitler,* p.686f.; Dörner, *Justiz*; see also Bormann's circular to the Gauleiter of 11.7.43 (IfZ, Party Chancellory, R33/43), in which he says, on Hitler's behalf, 'in the public treatment of the Jewish question every statement must remain subject to a future total solution'.
2 1919-PS, *IMT*, XXIX, p.110 ff. (4.10.43).
3 BAB, NS 36/13, published as PS-3063, *IMT*, XXXII, pp.20-23.

4 Kershaw, *Hitler*, p.767 ff. When this taboo was broken by Henriette von Schirach, the wife of the Gauleiter of Vienna, in June 1943, she was banished from Hitler's immediate circle. See Schirach, *Preis,* p.214f., and Schirach, *Ich glaubte an Hitler*, p.292f.
5 For details, see pp.182ff.

CHAPTER 2

1 Hitler, *Mein Kampf*, especially chapters 2, 3, 5 and 7. The possible influence of Vienna on Hitler and the difficulties of demonstrating this influence precisely are explained in Brigitte Hamann's study. The idea that Hitler first formed his world-view in Munich after the war can be found particularly in Joachimsthaler, *Weg*, and in Ian Kershaw's biography.
2 Lohalm, *Radikalismus*; Mosse, *Revolution, Handbuch.*
3 Hitler, *Aufzeichnungen*, no. 61.
4 Ibid., passim.
5 Ibid., cf. for example nos 100 (11.5.20), 112 (24.6.20), 136 (13.8.20, p.201), 416 (2.11.22,

p.720), 454 (speech of 3.1.23, p.779), 554 (5.8.23, p. 965).

6 Ibid., no. 91.

7 Ibid., no. 129.

8 Ibid., no. 116, Hitler to Konstantin Hierl.

9 Ibid., no. 223 (21.4.21). Baron Fisher of Kilverstone (1841–1920), British Admiral, First Sea Lord, 1914–15.

10 Ibid., no. 355 (2.2.22). For the genesis of the party programme see Kershaw, *Hitler*.

11 Ibid., no. 462 (18.1.23, p.796).

12 Hitler, book manuscript, published under the title 'Außenpolitische Standortsbestimmungen nach der Reichstagswahl, Juni-Juli 1928', in Hitler, *Reden*, IIA.

13 Ibid., p.183.

14 Jäckel, *Hitler's World View*, p.58f. cf. Hitler, *Mein Kampf:* '*wie die Made im faulenden Leib*' (p.61), '*Pestilenz, schlimmer als der schwarze Tod*', '*Bazillenträger schlimmster Art*' (p.62), '*ewiger Spaltpilz der Menschheit*' (p.135), '*Die Spinne begann, dem Volke langsam das Blut aus den Adern zu saugen*' (p.212) '*eine sich blutig bekämpfende Rotte von Ratten*' (p.331), '*Parasit im Körper anderer Völker*' (p.334), '*ein Schmarotzer, der wie ein schädlicher Bazillus sich immer mehr ausbreitet*' (p.334), '*den ewigen Blutegel*' (p.339), '*Völkerparasiten*' (p.358) '*Vampir*' (p.358).

15 Hitler, *Reden*, I, no. 7, speech in Weimar (4.7.1926); ibid., II/1,

no. 102, speech in Munich (9.4.1927); ibid., II/2, no 168, speech in Nuremberg (21.8.1927); ibid., II/2, no. 187, speech in Hof (16.10.2), p. 21; ibid., III/1, no. 2, speech in Berlin (13.7.1928), p.14f.; ibid., III/1, no. 24, speech in Bad Elster (14.9.1928), p.89f.; ibid., III/1, no. 37, speech in Oldenburg (18.10.1928), p.157ff.; ibid., III/3, no. 54, speech in Bautzen (6.6.1930).

16 Ibid. I, no.62, speech in Stuttgart (15.8.25); ibid., I, no. 72, speech in Wismar (8.10.25); ibid., II/1, no. 140, speech in Munich (3.6.27); ibid. II/1, no. 144, speech in Nuremberg, version A (9.6.27), p.363.

17 Ibid., II/1, no. 140, speech in Munich (3.6.27), p.340; ibid., II/1, no. 144, speech in Nuremberg, version A (9.6.27), p.363.

18 Ibid., II/1, no. 140, speech in Munich (3.6.27), p.340; ibid., II/1, no. 159, speech in Munich (30.7.27), p.434.

19 Ibid., I, no. 62, speech in Stuttgart (15.8.25), p.145; ibid. I, no. 72, speech in Wismar (8.10.25), p.172; ibid. II/1, no. 159, speech in Munich (30.7.27), p.428ff.

20 Ibid., I, no. 62, speech in Stuttgart (15.8.1925), p.145; ibid., I, no. 65, article in the *Völkischer Beobachter* (17.9.25), p.155; ibid., I, no. 72, speech in Wismar (8.10.25), p.172.

21 Ibid., I, no. 62, speech in Stuttgart (15.8.25), p.145; ibid., I, no. 72, speech in Wismar (8.10.25), p.172.
22 Ibid. II/1, no. 102, speech in Munich (9.4.27); ibid., II/1, no. 140, speech in Munich (3.6.27), p.340.
23 Ibid., III/1, no. 34, speech in Munich (10.10.28), p. 136; similar statement ibid., II/1, no. 153, speech in Freilassing (3.7.27).
24 Ibid., II/1, no. 159, speech in Munich (30.7.28), p. 433; ibid., III/1, no. 2, speech in Berlin (13.7.28); ibid., III/3, no. 14, article in the *Illustrierter Beobachter* (8.2.1930), p.81.
25 Ibid., I, no. 57, speech in Zwickau (15.7.1925), p.125; ibid., no. 34, speech in Munich (10.10.1928), p.143.
26 Ibid., I, no. 65, article in the *Völkischer Beobachter* (17.9.1925), p.153.
27 Ibid., II/1, no. 146, speech in Munich (13.6.1927), p.369.
28 Ibid., III/1, no. 39, speech in Augsburg (25.10.28), p.177; ibid., III/1, no. 61, speech in Nuremberg (3.11.28), p.307.
29 Ibid., II/1, no. 144, speech in Nuremberg (9.6.27), version A, p.363; ibid., II/1, no. 10, circular for the organisation of the Nazi Party in Austria (20.7.26), p.31.
30 Ibid., II/1, no. 159, speech in Munich (30.7.27), p.428; ibid., II/1, no. 235, speech in Munich (24.2.28), p.674; ibid., III/1, no.

13, speech in Munich (31.8.28), p.42.
31 Ibid., II/1, no. 159, speech in Munich (30.7.27), p.431.
32 Ibid., II/1, no. 235, speech in Munich (24.2.28), p.674. Similar statement, ibid., II/1, no. 159, speech in Munich (30.7.27), p.431.
33 Ibid., II/1, no. 159, speech in Munich (30.7.27), p.431.
34 Paul, *Aufstand*, p.236ff.
35 Hitler, *Reden*, IV/1, no. 29, speech in Bielefeld (16.1.30), p.110; ibid., IV/1, no. 96, speech in Kaiserslautern (26.4.31); ibid., IV/2, no. 67, speech in Gießen (9.11.31); ibid., IV/2, no. 70, speech in Darmstadt (13.11.31); ibid., IV/3, no. 4, speech in Lemgo (8.1.32).
36 Ibid., III/1, no. 97, speech at a Nazi Party rally in Munich (29.8.30), p.371.
37 Ibid., IV/1, no.14, speech in Munich (25.10.30), p.31.

CHAPTER 3

1 *Völkischer Beobachter*, 7.4.33.
2 Gruchmann, *Justiz*, p.126.
3 *Tagebücher Goebbels*, 26.3.33.
4 *Reichskanzlei/Regierung Hitler*, I/1, p.271.
5 *Völkischer Beobachter*, 7.4.33.
6 '*Gesetz zur Wiederherstellung des Berufsbeamtentums*' ['Law for the Restitution of the Professional Civil Service'], *RGBl*, I, 175; '*Gesetz über die Zulassung zur*

Rechtsanwaltschaft' ['Law concerning Admission to the Bar'], *RGBl*, I, 188.

7 '*Gesetz gegen die Überfüllung deutscher Schulen und Hochschulen*' ['Law against the Overpopulation of German Schools an Universities'], *RGBl*, I, 225.

8 See p.43f.

9 *Reichskanzlei/Regierung Hitler*, I/1, 323.

10 Ibid., I/1, p.629ff.

11 Longerich, *Politik*, p.46ff.

12 *Reichskanzlei/Regierung Hitler*, I/2, 865.

CHAPTER 4

1 Longerich, *Politik*, pp.47ff. and 53ff.

2 Ibid., p.70ff.

3 IfZ, Party-Chancellory, Rundschreiben R 164/35 (9.8.35); BAB, R 43II/602.

4 *Tagebücher Goebbels*, 14.9.38.

5 *Reichsministerium des Innern*.

6 *Parteitag der Freiheit*, p.113.

7 *Hitlers Denkschrift*.

8 RGBl 1936, I, 999 (1.12.36). Although the death penalty was never pronounced, in many instances lengthy prison terms were imposed (cf. Fischer, *Schacht*, p.199f.).

9 Barkai, *Boykott*, p.126f; details in: BAB, R 2/31.097. For this and the other two anti-Jewish legal proposals which were deferred, see Adam, *Judenpolitik*, p.159ff.

10 NG 4030, Memorandum from the Reichsfinanzministerium (25.4.38;) Genschel, *Vedrängung*, p.150f.

11 Decree of 12.11.38 (RGBl I, 1579).

12 Adam, *Judenpolitik*, p.100.

13 Ibid., p.165.

CHAPTER 5

1 *Reichstagung in Nürnberg 1937*, p.366ff.

2 Memorandum Clodius (Department of Trade) for *Referat Deutschland*, *ADAP*, series D, vol.5, no. 579 (28.1.38).

3 For the situation in spring 1938, see the summary in Longerich, *Politik*, p.155ff.

4 For details, see ibid., p.159ff.

5 OS, 500-1-261.

6 OS, 500-1-645, a note by Hagen from 30.6.38 on the discussion with Berndt as well as further material on this subject in the same file. For the speech by Goebbels, see *Völkischer Beobachter*, 21.6.38.

7 OS, 500-1-261 (29.6.38), letter to SD-Führer Oberabschnitt Süd. In the final copy corrected to 'on higher orders'.

8 *Tagebücher Goebbels*, 25.7.38.

9 For the background to the November pogrom, see the summary in Longerich, *Politik*, p.190ff.

10 *Völkischer Beobachter*, 9.11.38.

11 *Tagebücher Goebbels*, 10.11.38: 'in the afternoon the death of the

German diplomat vom Rath is
announced'.

12 Jordan, *Erlebt*, p.180.

13 In the study by Dröscher
(*Reichskristallnacht*), which is
based on the files of the
German Foreign Office, it
becomes clear (p.79f.) that the
news of the death must have
reached Hitler via Ribbentrop
before 8 p.m. and that the
Foreign Office was informed in
the course of the afternoon that
it was expected that he would
die on the same day.

14 *Tagebücher Goebbels*, 10.11.38.
The original phrase translated
by 'Things are ready now' is
uncertain. The fact that Hitler
had an intensive discussion with
Goebbels before he left the
room is confirmed by the testimony at Nuremberg by the
Chief of Police, von Eberstein:
IMT, XX, 320.

15 Reichspropagandaleiter (literally 'Director of Propaganda for
the Reich') was Goebbels' official function in the leadership
of the NSDAP.

16 BAB, NS 36/13, published in
IMT, XXXII, p.20ff.

17 *Adjutant*, see pp.228ff.;
Schallermeier (personal adjutant
on Himmler's staff), affidavit,
5.7.46: SS-(A)-5, IMT XLII,
p.511ff.

18 On the reporting by the Nazi
press, see Obst, *Reichskristallnacht*,
p.65f. and Benz, *Rückfall*, p.14ff.
Concerning the damage, see

Popplow, *Novemberpogrom*; the
report of Oberstaatsanwalt
Eisenach on the destruction of a
shop between 9 and 10.11.38,
published in Pätzold/Runge,
Kristallnacht, p.125ff.; a first
attempt to set fire to the synagogue in Windecken was made
as early as 9.11 – see Kingreen,
Landleben, p.132; Kropat,
Kristallnacht, p.27, for the whole
of Hessen on 9.11.38.

19 BAB, NS 36/13, published in
IMT, XXXII, pp.20-29.

20 *Tagebüche Goebbels*, 11.11.38.

21 Telegram, 2.56 a.m., BAB, BDC
Schumacher Collection, 240/I.

22 Telex, 11.56 p.m., 374PS, published in *IMT*, XXV, 377;
telegram, 1.20 a.m., 3051-PS,
published ibid., XXXI, pp.516ff.

23 For details see Heydrich's fig-
ures at the meeting on 12.11.38
(note 30) and the report of the
Highest Party Court (note 93).
For details of the pogrom itself
and its effects, see in particular
Obst, *Reichskristallnacht* and
Longerich, *Politik*, p.202ff.

24 According to Göring in the
discussion of 6 December (next
note).

25 Published in: Aly/Heim,
Ordnung.

26 Announced by order of the
Führer's Deputy, no. 1/39 g,
17.1.39, 069-PS, *IMT*, XXV,
131ff. ('On my advice, the
Führer has made the following
decisions relating to the Jewish
question…').

27 *Sonderrecht* (Walk), III, 154.

28 *RGBl* 1939, I, 864.

29 *RMBliV* 1291, 16.6.39.

30 1816-PS, *IMT*, XXVIII, p.499ff.

31 For the origins of the Schacht plan, see Weingarten, *Hilfeleistung*, p.127ff.; Fischer, *Schacht*, p.216ff.

32 Schacht was given consent during a talk with Hitler in Munich: *ADAP*, series D, vol. 5, no. 654, undated note to the draft of a telegram by Wiehl, 12.12.38.

33 BAB, 25-01, 6641, Rublee's note to Schacht on 23.11.38 with the outline of the project. Details of the plan and the negotiations are in a note by Schacht, 16.1.39, ibid., published in *ADAP*, series C, vol. 5, no. 661. See also Weingarten, *Hilfeleistung*, p.135ff.

34 1816-PS, *IMT*, XXVIII, p.499ff.

35 *ADAP*, series D, vol. 4, no. 271.

36 *ADAP*, series D, vol. 4, no. 158.

37 Speech made on January 30, published in Domarus, *Hitler*, II, p.1047ff. (the passage cited here, p.1055-58).

CHAPTER 6

1 BAB, NS 18alt/842.

CHAPTER 7

1 Jansen/Weckbecker, *Selbstschutz*; the main objectives of the German occupational policy in Poland are explained in Broszat, *Polenpolitik*, and more recently in Majer, *Fremdvölkische*.

2 Memorandum Oberstleutnant Lahousen, published in Groscurth, *Tagebücher*, p.357ff.

3 *IMT*, XXXIX, p.425ff., 172-USSR, statement by Hitler from 2.12.39.

4 *Diensttagebuch*, 30.5.40

5 This was the title of a publication by the psychiatrist Alfred Hoche and the lawyer Karl Binding. On the background to 'euthanasia', see Friedlander, *Origins*, p.1ff.; Faulstich, *Hungersterben*.

6 Hitler, *Reden*, II/1, nos 4.9.29; 7.9.29; Klee, *Euthanasie*, pp.31f. & 52.

7 Literature on the euthanasia programme in the annexed Polish districts includes Rieß, *Anfänge*; Bernhardt, *Antaltspsychiatrie*; Aly, *Final Solution*, p.70ff.

8 Literature on children's euthanasia includes Friedlander, *Origins*, p.37ff.; Klee, *Euthanasie*, p.77ff.; Burleigh, *Death*, p.93ff.; and Schmuhl, *Rassenhygiene*, p.182.

9 Literature on the *T-4 Aktion* includes Burleigh, *Death*, p.111ff.; Friedlander, *Origins*, p.62ff.; Klee, *Euthanasie*, p.82ff.; and Schmuhl, *Rassenhygiene*, p.190ff.

10 BAB, R22/4209.

CHAPTER 8

1   BAB, R 58/825, 15.9.1939.
2   BAB, R 58/825,
    Amtschefbesprechungen, minutes
    of 27.9.39.
3   *Politisches Tagebuch*, p.81.
4   *Staatsmänner und Diplomaten*, I,
    p.29f. (26.9.39).
5   *ADAP*, series D, vol. 8, no. 176,
    p.143ff., minutes of 2.10.39.
6   *Vertrauliche Information* (Bulletin
    of the Ministry of Propaganda),
    9.10.41, published in
    Hagemann, *Presselenkung*, p.145.
7   *Verhandlungen des Reichstages*,
    vol. 460, p.51ff.
8   *IMT*, XXVI, p.255f., 686-PS.
9   YV, 053/87, note by Günther,
    11.10.39.
10 Memorandum of the
    'Sonderbeauftragte', 10.10.39
    (not preserved in the original,
    excerpt prepared *post factum*),
    cited in Botz, *Wohnungspolitik*,
    p.105, from the Österreichisches
    Staatsarchiv.
11 YV, 053/87, note from the
    Gestapo outpost in Mährisch-
    Ostrau, 21.10.39.
12 *IMT*, XXVI, p.378f., 864-PS,
    minute of 20.10.39. For the
    doubts on the part of the mili-
    tary about further concentra-
    tion of Jews in the area of
    Lublin, see also the note by
    Krüger on 1.11, *Diensttagebuch*,
    p.56.

CHAPTER 9

1   The document (and Himmler's
    commentary) is published in
    VfZ, 5 (1957), 194-198 (with a
    short introduction by Helmut
    Krausnick).
2   *Die Judenfrage im Friedensvertrage*
    ['The Jewish Question in the
    Peace Treaty'], 9.7.41 (Inland
    IIg 177, published in *ADAP*,
    series D, vol. 10, no. 101,
    p.92ff.). See also Rademacher's
    note of 2.7.40, *Plan zur Lösung
    der Judenfrag* ['Plan for the
    Solution of the Jewish
    Question'], ibid.
3   Summarised in a Brochure:
    PAA, Inland IIg 177.
4   Ibid., *Die Judenfrage im
    Friedensvertrage*.
5   Ibid., *Plan zur Lösung der
    Judenfrage*.
6   Ciano, *Tagebücher*, p.249;
    Schmidt, *Statist*, p.494f.
7   *Lagevorträge Oberbefehlshabers
    Kriegsmarine*, p.106ff.
8   *Diensttagebuch*, 12.7.40.
9   PAA, Inland IIg 177, note by
    Luther (15.8.1940); published in
    ADAP, series D, vol. 10, no. 345:
    'he intends to evacuate all the
    Jews from Europe after the war'.
10 *Tagebücher Goebbels*, 17.8.40.

CHAPTER 10

1   Toury, *Entstehungsgeschichte*,
    p.143; Adler, *Mensch*, p.115ff.

2 In a draft for a letter on
   7.12.40, Rademacher changed
   the wording 'deportation
   ordered by Führer' to 'deportation approved by Führer' (PAA,
   Inland IIg 189; Toury,
   Entstehungsgeschichte, p.443).

3 Halder, *Kriegstagebuch,* vol. 2
   (4.11.40).

4 *Tagebücher Goebbels*, 5.11.40,
   referring to the previous day.

5 Numbers based on Polish sources
   and research in *Okkupationspolitik
   Polen*, p.356f.

6 *IMT*, XXIX, p.176f., 1950-PS,
   letter from Lammers to von
   Schirach (3.12.40).

7 Safrian, *Eichmann-Männer*, p.97f;
   Adler, *Mensch*, p.147ff. with further details.

8 CDJC, V-59, published in
   Klarsfeld, *Vichy*, p.361ff.

9 Published in Adler, *Mensch*, p.152.

10 Safrian, *Eichmann-Männer*, p.97

11 *Tagebücher Goebels*, 18.3.41.

12 *Diensttagebuch*, 25.3.41.

13 Ibid., 3.4.41.

14 Decisive for this are Hitler's
   orders no. 18 ('Russia') from
   12.11.40 and no. 21 from
   18.12.41 ('The Barbarossa
   Case'), published in *Hitler's
   Weisungen*.

15 Aly, *Final Solution*, p.172.

16 PAA, Inland IIg 177 (copy),
   IMT, XXVI, 710-PS.

17 For details see Gerlach, *Morde*,
   p.44ff.

18 *Tagebücher Goebbels,*, 20.6.41,
   referring to the previous day.

19 *Diensttagebuch*.

20 *ADAP*, series D, vol. 13, no.
   207.

CHAPTER 11

1 *Kriegstagebuch OKW 1*, 341.

2 BAM, RW 19/185.

3 *Kriegstagebuch OKW 1* 341.

4 BAM, RW 4/v. 522 (=*IMT*,
   XXVI, p.53ff., 447-PS).

5 *Kriegstagebuch* (Halder) II,
   pp.317ff. & 320.

6 Ibid., p.335ff

7 BAM, RH 22/155; RH 22082;
   RH 22/12; RH 22/155.
   Published in Jacobsen,
   Kommissarbefehl, nos 8, 12, 11, 3.

8 IfZ; NOKW 2079, published in
   Jacobsen, *Kommissarbefehl*, document 9.

9 All leading members of the
   Einsatzgruppen that were asked
   about this after the war testified
   that these special units received
   orders for the mass murder of
   the Jewish civilian population in
   the occupied parts of the Soviet
   Union during the course of the
   spring or summer of 1941. These
   testimonies do contain inconsis-
   tent information about the time,
   place and precise contents of
   these orders, and the claim by
   most unit commanders that the
   indiscriminate liquidation of the
   whole Jewish population,
   including women and children,
   had been ordered before the
   beginning of the war seems
   unreliable, since it is probably an

element in a defence strategy designed for circumstances in which a defendant claims he had carry out orders from a superior in all possible circumstances. Despite these reservations, it is remarkable that the order to carry out mass murder is not in principle denied in any of the testimonies. Details in Longerich, *Politik*, p.315ff.

10 BAB, R 70 SU/32, published in Longerich, *Ermordung*, p.118ff.

11 BAB, R 70 SU/32, published ibid., p.116ff.

12 BAB, R 58/214-221.

13 For details see Longerich, *Politik*, p.321ff.

14 Report of 15.10.41 (Stahlecker-Bericht), 180-L, *IMT*, XXXVII, p.670ff.

15 For the pogrom in Kovno, see the various witness statements in *Those were the days*, p.23ff.; EM 8 and Tory, *Surviving*, pp.7ff.

16 EM 9; Arad, *Getto*, p.46.

17 On Riga see also EM 15. See also ZSt, II 207 AR-Z 7/59, Judgement Landgericht(=LG, district court) Hamburg.

18 Arad, *Getto*, p.46 (Siauliai); EM 40, Ezergailis, *Holocaust*, pp.156ff. (Jelgava).

19 See note 14.

20 EM 24; Roth, *Heydrichs Professor*, pp.289ff.

21 EM 14 from 6.7.41, and EM 47.

22 Pohl, *Ostgalizien*, p.54ff. and Musial, *Elemente*, p.172. Musial does not give sufficient weight

to initiatives for pogroms that stemmed from the German side.

23 EM 112.

24 EM 81 and EM 112.

25 EM 19.

26 *Sonderkommando* (SK, special commando) 1b: Dvinsk, 1150 victims (EM 24, Ezergailis, *Holocaust*, p.271ff.); *Einsatzkommando* (EK, operational commando) 2 Riga, 2,000 victims, some murdered by the Latvian auxiliary police (EM 24); Jelgava, 160 victims, some of whom were women and children (ZSt, II 207 AR 1779/66, Judgement LG Dortmund, 8.7.88); at the beginning of July EK 3 organised mass shootings (Jäger-report 1.12.41, OS, 500-1-25) in the fortifications of the city of Kovno; according to Jäger's list, 2,930 Jewish men and 47 women were shot. From 7 July, Jäger went on, a group of men from his unit 'in cooperation with the Lithuanian partisans' also began to carry out mass executions outside of Kovno, in the course of which, in the month of July, over 1,400 people, overwhelmingly Jewish men, were murdered.

27 On 24, 25 and 27 June, in Garsden, Krottingen and Polangen (immediately across the border with Lithuania) the unit executed 201, 214 and 111 civilians respectively, the vast majority of whom were Jewish

men (OS, 500-1-758, telex from the Gestapo office in Tilsit from 1.7.41, and EM 14). During the following days further 'cleansing actions' followed, in which, according to the situation report of 18 July, 3302 people had been shot (EM 19, EM 24 and EM 26; see also Judgement LG Ulm from 29.8.58, published in *Justiz*, no. 465). The fact that in the reports of the many shootings carried out later in the border areas only the deaths of women, old men and children are noted, but not those of men of military age, is evidence that all Jewish men of this age-group had indeed been murdered in the first wave of shootings (see p.71).

28 SK 7a: Vileyka, end of June/beginning of July, 'the whole of male Jewry was liquidated' (EM 50); Vitebsk, end of July/beginning of August, 332 victims (EM 50; Judgement LG Essen of 29.3.65, published in *Justiz* XX, no. 588); SK 7b: Borisov, July, and in the area of Orsha/Mogilev, end of July beginning of August (Ogorreck, *Einsatzgruppen*, p.116ff); EK 8: Bialystok, beginning of July, two 'actions' with at least 800 and 100 victims respectively, and Baranovichi, July, two executions each with at least 100 victims; Minsk end of July and August, when more than 1,000 Jews were killed

(LG Munich, I from 21.7.61, published in *Justiz*, XVII, no. 519, p.672ff.; Judgement LG Kiel of 8.4.64, published in *Justiz*, XIX, no. 567, p.790ff.; ZSt, 202 AR-Z 81/59, vol. 1, Indictment of 19.4.60); Slonim, middle of July, 1,075 victims (EM 32, Judgement LG Cologne of 12.5.64, published in *Justiz*, XX, no. 573, p.171ff.); EK 9: Vilna, together with the Lithuanian auxiliary police, in July at least 4,000 5,000 victims (Judgement LG Berlin of 22.6.62, published in *Justiz*, XVIII, no. 540a); 10,000 people were presumed shot (Zst, 207 AR-Z 14/58, note referring to Ek 3, 27.9.61, Korrespondenz-Akte, 6, p.1151ff.).

29 EK 6: Dobromil, 30.6, at least 80 victims (ZSt, 204 AR 1258/66, Indictment of 30.1.68 and Judgement LG Tübingen, 31.7.1969); EK 5 and 6: Lvov, according to the events report of 16.7 'about 7,000' (EM 24, see also Ogorreck, *Einsatzgruppen*, p.142ff., Pohl, *Ostgalizien*, p.60ff., Held Pogrom, Roth, *Heydrichs Professor*, p.289f.; EK 5: Berdichev and surrounding areas, e.g. Chmielnik, July, 299 victims (EM 47); Ek 6: Vinnitsa, second half of July, two executions with 146 and 600 victims (EM 38, 47 and 86); SK 4a: Sokal, end of June more than 300 victims (EM 24; ZSt, 114

AR-Z 269/60, final report SK
4 a, 30.12.64, 150 and
Judgement, 29.11.68; Ogorreck,
Einsatzgruppen, p.130ff.); Lutsk,
end of June/beginning of July,
approx. 2,000 Jews (EM 14);
Zitomir, July, three 'actions'
with over 600 Jewish men, 7
August, a further 402 victims
(ZSt, 114 AR-Z 269/60, final
report SK 4a, 30.12.1964). SK
4b:Vinnitsa, second half of July,
at least 100 victims (ibid.).

30 EM 17, 9.7.41. The unit
reported in EM 43 from 5.8.41,
'between 21.-31.7.41 3,947
people were liquidated'.

31 SK 10a: Kodyma, 1.8.1941, 98
victims (MA, RH 20/11-488,
Ogorreck, *Einsatzgruppen*, p.153f.
and Krausnick,
Einsatzgruppen/Truppe, p.238f.); SK
10b: Czernowitz, participation in
massacre of Rumanian troops, 8
and 9.7.41, 100 victims (NOKW
587 and 3453, see also Ogorreck,
Einsatzgruppen, p.154f.. At the end
of July EG D reported that in the
city, 'of about 1,200 Jews arrested,
682 were shot in collaboration
with the Rumanian police' (EM
45); SK 11a: Kishinev, up to the
beginning of August 'so far 551
Jews' had been shot (EM 45); SK
11b:Tighina, 7.8.41, 155 victims
(EM 45; StA Munich, 115 Ks Ga-
c 71, Indictment of 19.8.71); EK
12: Babtschinsky, 20 and 21.7.41,
94 victims (EM 61; StA Munich
119 c Js 1/69, Indictment of
28.10.72).

32 Polizeibataillon 309: on 27 June
the battalion had already carried out a massacre in Bialystok
in which at least 2,000 Jews,
including women and children,
were killed. Members of the
battalion drove at least 500
people into the synagogue and
murdered them by setting fire
to the building (Judgement LG
Wuppertal 24.5.73, ZSt,V 205
ARZ 20/60). Polizeibataillon
316: Baranovichi, second half of
July, several hundred dead (ZSt,
II 202 AR-Z 168/59, disposition of the public prosecutor
Dortmund, 8.11.68; Judgement
LG Freiburg of 12.7.63, published in *Justiz*, XIX, no. 555;
Polizeibataillon 307: Brest-
Litovsk, 12.7., several thousand
Jewish civilians (note, public
prosecutor's office Lübeck,
9.9.65, ZSt, AR-Z 82/61).

33 Also in EM 26. On Himmler's
journey see also the diary of his
personal assistant, Brandt, 30.6
(BAB, NS 19/3957).

34 OS, 500-1-25 (also ZSt, Dok. SU
401). On this, also EM 11 (SPSD
= *Sicherheitspolizei* and SD).

35 EM 21 of 13.7.1941; ZSt, II 202
AR 72a/60, Judgement LG
Berlin of 6.5.66.

36 On the visits of 30.6 and 9.7,
see Brandt's engagement diary
(BAB, NS 19/3957) and the
diary of Bach-Zelewski (BAB,
R 20/45b).

37 For details see Longerich,
Politik, p.349ff.

38 YV 053/127, Kriegstagebuch
    (KTB, war diary), Police
    Battalion 322, 9.7.41.
39 YV 053/128, file relating to
    KTB.Pol.Btl. 322.
40 YV 053/127, KTB Pol.Btl. 322,
    8.7.41.
41 Angrick et al., *Tagebuch*,
    p.334ff.; Judgement of the
    Landgericht Bochum against
    members of Police Battalion
    316 also involved in this mas-
    sacre (LG Bochum of 6.6.68,
    ZSt, II 202 AR.-Z 168/59).

CHAPTER 12

1 221-L, *IMT*, XXXVIII, p.86ff.
2 Kriegstagebuch of the unit
   staff, published in *Unsere Ehre*,
   p.30. The cavalry brigade was
   not formally constituted until 2
   August, from two cavalry regi-
   ments.
3 Final Report of 13.8.41, published in *Unsere Ehre*, p.224ff.;
   Förster, *Gesicht*, p.160.
4 STA Wolfenbüttel, 62 Nds Fb.2,
   1268.
5 Judgement LG Berlin, 22.6.62
   (published in *Justiz*, XVIII, no.
   540); ZSt, II 202 AR 72a/60,
   Judgement LG Berlin, 6.5.66.
   On EK 9 see Ogorreck,
   Einsatzgruppen, p.186ff.
6 ZSt, 202 AR-Z 73/61, vol. 6,
   p.1580ff., 22.2.1966; see also the
   interrogation of Filbert on
   23.9.71 (ZSt, 201 AR-Z 76/59,
   vol. 11, p.7563ff.).

7 ZSt, 201 AR-Z 76/59, 8.10.71
   (vol. 11, p.7605ff.).
8 At another point Bradfisch said
   that the same information had
   been given him by Himmler
   later in Mogilev: StA München,
   22 Ks 1/1961, vol. 1, 136ff.,
   22.4.58.
9 Bobruisk, probably in the first
   half of September, with at least
   400 victims (EM 90; Judgement
   LG München I, 21.7.61, published in *Justiz*, XVII, no. 519;
   ZSt, 202 AR-Z 81/59,
   Indictment of 19.4.60); Borisov,
   beginning of September until
   October, various 'actions' (ibid.,
   and EM 108); Lahoisk, first half
   of September, 920 victims,
   meaning that the place was
   then 'free of Jews' (judenfrei)
   according to EM 90; see also
   Judgement LG Cologne,
   12.5.64, published in *Justiz*,
   XX, no. 573); Smolevichi, end
   of September, 1,401 victims
   according to EM 108 (see also
   Judgement LG Cologne,
   12.5.64, published in *Justiz*, XX,
   no. 573).
10 YV 053/127, *Kriegstagebuch
   Polizeibataillon 322*, 29.8.1941 and
   1.9.1941. On the shootings in
   Minsk, see also the witness testimony of Alois Fischer,
   27.10.1965 (ZSt, AR-Z 6/65,
   vol. 2, p.484ff.) and Friedrich
   Soier, 19.10.1965 (ibid., p.383ff.).
11 Ibid., STA Minsk, 655-1-1 (copy
   USHM, Minsk-collection, role
   4), a note on a document on the

course to be taken for the 'fighting against partisans', 25 and 26.9.1941. See also witness testimony Nagel, commander of the Battalion, ZSt, AR–Z 52/59, Sonderbd. 2, p.318f. cf. Angrick et al., *Tagebuch*, p.345f.

12 In Mogilev, on 2 October, '2,208 Jews of both sexes' were shot; and on 19 October '3,726 Jews of both sexes and all ages' were shot (EM 135 and EM 133; Angrick et.al., *Kriegstagebuch*, p.346ff.; YV053/27, *Kriegstagebuch Polizeibataillon* 322, 2/3.10.41; Judgement LG Munich I, 21.7.61, published in *Justiz*, XVII, no. 519; ZSt, 202 AR–Z 81/59, Indictment of 19.4.60; Judgement LG Kiel, 8.4.64, published in *Justiz*, XIX, no. 567).

13 Activity and Situation Report no. 8, no. 2659 (for Bobruisk, Vitebsk and Gomel, published in *Einsatzgruppen Sowjetunion*, pp. 263ff.). On Bobruisk: ZSt, 202 AR–Z 81/59, Indictment of 19.4.60 and Judgement LG Munich, 21.7.61. On Borisov, see Wilhelm, *Einsatzgruppe A/Truppe*, p.576ff.

14 EM 133.

15 NOKW 1165, report by HSSPF South to AOK 6, 1.8.41 on the 'cleansing action' (*Säuberungsaktion*) from 28.7 to 30.7.41; BAM, RH 22/5, order to go into action issued by Jeckeln on 25.7.41; after this, suspicious 'female agents or Jews' were to be 'treated accordingly'.

16 Activity-report of the 1st SS-Brigade, 30.7.41 for the period 27.7 to 30.7 (*Unsere Ehre*, pp. 197ff.). See also BAB, NS 33/39 Report 1st SS Brigade, 30.7.41, on this period. Also, ibid., NS 33/22, Activity-report of the unit staff, RFSS, 6.8.41 for the period 28.7 to 3.8.41.

17 Thus on 4.8.41 1109 Jewish men and 275 Jewish women (activity-report 1st SS-Brigade for the period from 3.8 to 6.8.41, published in *Unsere Ehre*, p.108f.; see also Spector, *Holocaust*, p.76f., with more details); on 7.8.41, 232 Jews in Tschernjachov (activity-report of the 1st Brigade from 6.8 to 10.8 made on 10.8.41, published in *Unsere Ehre*, p.111ff.); around 20.8, 300 Jewish men and 139 Jewish women in Starokonstantinov (EM 59 from 21.8.41) and in the period from 2 to 7.9.41 '1,009 Jews and Red-Army members' (BAB, NS 33/22, report by the unit staff on their activity between 1.9 and 7.9, made on 10.9.41).

18 EM 60; BAB, NS 33/22, Jeckeln's reports to the Chief of Staff, 27.8 to 30.8.41. See also the account in Braham, *Kamenets Podolsk*.

19 197-PS, minute of 27.8.41.

20 In early September, '1,303 Jews, including 876 women over the age of 12', were executed (EM 88); see also BAB, NS 33/22, telex HSSPF South, 5.9.

21 19.9.41, more than 3,000 victims (EM 106).

22 29.9.41, 33,771 victims (according to EM 106). For Babi Yar, see Rieß, *Massaker, Schoáh* (Wien).

23 13.10.41 'approx. 10,000' victims (according to EM 135).

24 Details in Longerich, *Politik*, pp.376ff.

25 Judgement LG Darmstadt, 29.11.1968. On the shootings in Belaja Cercov see also the testimony of the Luftwaffe soldier Friedrich Wilhelm Liebe, 14.6.1665 (IfZ, Gd 01.54, 49). The whole process is documented in detail in: *Those were the Days*, p.137ff.

26 Fastov, August, 'all the Jews from the ages of 12 to 60, in total 252 heads' (EM 80, 11.9.41; ZSt, 114 AR-Z 269/60, final report, 30.12.68). Further massacres include Radomyschl, 6.9, 1,668 victims (Judgement LG Darmstadt, 29.11.68 and EM 88); Zitomir, several shootings in August, including 3,145 victims on 19.8 alone (EM 106).

27 Boguslav, 15.9, 322 victims, which is to say all the inhabitants of the town; Uman, 22 to 23.9 (according to information from the unit, 1,412 victims); Cybulow, 25.9, 70 victims, Perejeslas, 4.10, 537 victims, Koshewatoje, 'all the Jews in the town' (all details from EM 119). See also the summary information on the murders perpe-

trated by EK 5 in EM 111 (8,800 Jewish victims) and EM 132 (15,110 victims in all).

28 ZSt, 201 AR-Z 76/59, vol. 6, p.58ff., 22.3.1971. See also ibid., vol. 2, p.375f., 7.2.1957, ibid., vol. 4, application for prior investigation, 29.12.1969. On this see also 204 AR-Z 266/59, Indictment of 30.12.1964. On the questioning of Schulz, see also Ogorreck, *Einsatzgruppen*, p.190ff.

29 Teilkommando Kronberger (EM 135); *Dienstkalender*.

30 First near Kovel on 22 July: ZSt, 204 AR-Z 1251/65 D, Schlußvermerk Bayerisches Landeskriminalamt 19.12.77. In addition, reports BAB, NS 33/22, telexes HSSPF South of 21.8, 24.8, 27.8 with reports on shootings by Battalion 314.

31 Shepetovka (end of July, all Jewish inhabitants); Slavuta (552 victims); Sudylkov (471 dead) and Berdishev (1,000 victims): ZSt, II 204 AR-Z 1251/65; BAB, NS 33/22 telex HSSPF Russia South, 19.8 (for Slavuta).

32 Statement of Nosske, 9.4.62 (StA Munich, 119 c Js 1/69, vol. 4, p.482ff.); statement of Max Drexel, 17.4.62 (vol. 2, p.132ff.), statement of Karl Becker, 22.9.61 (vol. 3, p.274ff.) as well as the statement of Erwin Harsch, 1.12.47 (vol. 7, p.1604ff.). Cf. also Ogorreck, *Einsatzgruppen*, p.157ff.

33 Ananjew, SK 10b, 28.8 'about
   300 Jews and Jewesses', i.e. all
   the Jews in the town, were shot
   (NOKW 1702, report of 3.9.41;
   no. 4992, testimony by Robert
   Barth, 12.9.47); Dubossary, EK
   12, in the middle of September
   all the Jewish inhabitants, about
   1,500 people, and 1,000 Jews
   from the surrounding towns
   were murdered in two actions
   (StA Munich, 119 c Js 1/69,
   Indictment, 28.10.70 and
   Judgement LG Munich,
   18.11.74); Nikolajew, SK 11a,
   end of September, all the
   inhabitants of the ghetto, about
   5,000 people (StA Munich, 119
   c Js 1/69), Indictment
   28.10.70); Cherson, SK 11 a,
   end of September beginning of
   October, all the Jewish inhabitants (StA Munich, 118 Ks 268,
   Indictment, 8.3.66; BAM, RH
   20-11/488, report on the activity of SK 11a in Cherson from
   22.8 to 10.9.41).

34 ZSt, II 213 AR 1902/66,
   Hauptakte XI, questioning of
   Nosske, 13.3.69, p.2610ff.; similarly also ZSt, II 213 AR
   1902/66, Korrespondenz-Akte,
   vol. 2, p.597ff., 24.5.71; questioning of Drexel, 17.4.62
   (ibid., 2, p.132ff.); on the testimony of Nosske, see Ogorreck,
   Einsatzgruppen, p.207ff.

35 Breitman, *Architect*, p.213f.;
   BAB, NS 19/3957.

36 EM 95, EM 116; activity and
   situation report no. 6, no. 2656

(published in *Einsatzgruppen
Sowjetunion*, pp.222ff. & 232).

37 Jäger-Bericht, OS, 500-1-25;
   Judgement LG Ulm, 29.8.58,
   published in *Justiz*, XV, no. 465.

38 This unit had already liquidated
   18,000 Jews, or had them shot
   by Latvian auxiliaries at the
   beginning of September (EM
   96).

39 See footnote 206.

40 Gerlach, *Morde*, p.46ff.

41 BAB, R 43II/687a, Lammers to
   Rosenberg, 6.9.41.

42 See pp.209ff.

43 OS, 500-1-25, copy in ZSt,
   Dok. UdSSR no. 401.

44 Browning, *Final Solution*, p.74.

CHAPTER 13

1 Note for Frick on Eichmann's
   announcement in the Ministry
   of Propaganda, 15.8.41, published in: *Reichsministerium*,
   p.303.

2 *Tagebücher Goebbels*, 19.8.41.

3 BAB, NS 19/2655, published in
   Ermordung (Longerich), p.157.

4 BAB, R 6/34a, note by
   Koeppen.

5 *Monologe*, 25.10.41.

6 Trial Eichmann, doc. 1544,
   Heydrich to Himmler, 19.10.41.

7 *Kriegstagebuch Bräutigam*, p.144.

8 Longerich, *Politik*, p.432f.

9 Ibid., p.431f.

10 BAB, R 6/34a, 21.9.41.

11 There is no documentary evidence for the thesis that Hitler

decided in summer 1941 to
murder all the European Jews,
as it is put forward by Hilberg,
Aktion Reinhard and Breitmann,
Architect (who only sees here the
implementation of a fundamental decision taken earlier).
Because of the chronology, close
investigation does not support
statements often used in this
context, such as that by Höß
claiming that Himmler had
passed on a decision to this
effect made by the Führer in
summer 1941 (Commandant,
p.1837ff.), or that by Eichmann
maintaining that an order with
the same content had been
passed to him in September or
October by Heydrich (*Trial
Eichmann*,VII, p.169ff.).
Heyrich's 'authorisation' by
Göring on 31.7.41 to make
'preparations' for a 'complete
solution of the Jewish Question'
in Europe (710-PS, *IMT*, XXVI,
p.266ff.), refers to the plan for
deportations, and is not the
instruction to commit mass
murder in gas chambers. For
details, see Longerich, *Politik*,
p.421ff.The thesis that Hitler
made his decision in autumn
1941 is similarly not sufficiently
documented. See below, p.79.

12 *Tagebücher Goebbels*, 24.9.41.

13 SUA, 114-2-56 (also YV, M 58/23),
published in *Protektorátní*, no. 15.

14 Heyrich will have meant camps
for civilian prisoners, such as
those in Minsk and Mogilew

(cf. Gerlach, *Failure*, p.62).

15 Compiled from data in the fol-
lowing sources:YV, JM 10.731,
Arolsen International Tracing
Service; Arndt/Boberach,
Deutsches Reich, p.44f.; Arndt,
Luxemburg, in *Dimension*, pp.95-
104; Moser, *Österreich*, p.76;
Schmidt-Hartmann,
Tschechoslowakei, p.361; Safrian,
Eichmann-Männer, p.120f.;
Report by the Inspector of the
German uniformed Police
Lodz (13.11.41), published in
DiM (Lodz) I, p.203ff.;
Matzerath, *Weg*, p.536f.

16 Compiled from data in the fol-
lowing sources:YV, JM 10.731,
Arolsen International Tracing
Service; Arndt/Boberach,
Deutsches Reich, p.47; Moser,
Österreich, p.79; Adler,
Theresienstadt, p.50.

17 Schneider, *Journey*.

18 Compiled from data in the fol-
lowing sources:YV, JM 10.731,
Arolsen International Tracing
Service; Arndt/Boberach,
Deutschland, p.46; Moser, Öster-
reich, p.79; Schmidt-Hartmann,
Tschechoslowakei, p.361.

19 IFZ, Fb 95, 27, Note
Gotenhafen, 24.10.41, Summary
of a discussion with Eichmann.

20 Longerich, *Politik*, p.448ff.

21 CDJC, I-28, already published
in Klarsfeld, *Vichy*, p.369ff.

22 See Zeitschel's account of
22.8.41, CDJC,V-15, published
in Klarsfeld, *Vichy*, p.367f. and
14.9.41, CDJC,VI 126.

23 The meeting took place on
16.9.41 (*Dienstkalender*). Zeitschel
informed Dannecker of the content of this conversation on
8.10.41: CDJC,V-16, published
in Klarsfeld, *Endlösung*, p.25. For
Zeitschel's recommendations
during this period see the extensive account in Witte, *Decisions*,
pp.327ff.

24 This can be seen from his two
notes of 22.8.41 and 14.9.41
(see footnote 22).

25 Klarsfeld, *Vichy*, pp.25 and 28ff.;
Herbert, *Militärverwaltung*,
p.435ff.

26 Herbert, *Militärverwaltung*, esp.
pp.438f. and 448f.

27 Klarsfeld, *Vichy*, p.34ff.

28 BAB, NS 19/1734.

29 PAA, Inland IIg 194, 28.10.41,
published in *ADAP*, series D,
vol. 13, no. 725, p.570ff.

30 The view that Hitler had
already taken a clear decision
on the European Jews in
autumn 1941 is represented particularly by Christopher
Browning (lastly in *Policy*, p.33)
and Burrin, *Hitler*, p.115ff.

31 *Reichsgesetzblatt* 1941, I, 547; see
also the memo of the Ministry
of the Interior from 15.9.41
with guidelines for the execution of the police instructions
of 1.9.41 (*Dokumente Verfolgung*,
p.207ff.). See also Hilberg,
Destruction, p.177ff.

32 *Tagebücher Goebbels*, 19.8.41,
referring to a conversation held
on the previous day.

33 Decree of 4.11.41; see Walk,
Sonderrecht, IV, 261.

34 *RGBl* 1941, I, p.722ff.

35 Order of the Reich Interior
Ministry of 3.12, no. 5336, published in Adler, *Mensch*, p.503f.
and commentary, ibid., p.491ff.

36 CDJC, XXVb-7. On this general topic, see Adler, *Mensch*,
p.29ff.

37 PAA, Pol.Abt. III 245; see
Browning, *Solution*, p.66.

38 On this see PAA, Inland IIg
174, Luther's request to the
German missions in the three
countries from 10.11.1941. The
agreement of the Rumanian,
Croatian and Slovakian governments was received by telex
from the German Heads of
Mission in Bucharest, Agram
and Preßburg on 13.11.1941,
20.11.1941 and 4.12.1941.
Luther informed Eichmann
about the results of his efforts
on 10.1.1941. See Browning,
Solution, p.67f.

CHAPTER 14

1 Friedlander, *Origins*, p.111ff.
2 See p.145f.
3 no. 365, published in Krausnick,
Judenverfolgung, p.337f. Wetzel
wrote that there were 'no reservations' about using 'Brack's
useful aids' for the murder of
Central European Jews who
were not capable of working.
Wetzel was obviously not com-

pletely informed about the
politices of the RSHA, which
at this point had not yet begun
to make direct plans for the
murder of the Central
European Jews. The fact that
the Security Police in the Baltic
States also shot 6,000 Jews from
Germany in November 1941, in
contravention of the 'guidelines' of the RSHA could also
be partly due to Wetzel's false
information. See below, p.87.

4 This process was reconstructed
on the basis of witness statements. See Beer, *Entwickung*,
p.407; Staatsanwaltschaft
München, Anklage gegen Karl
Wolff (ZSt, ASA 137).

5 Beer, *Entwicklung*, p.408: state-
ment by Widmann of 11.1.60,
202 ARZ 152/159, p.33ff;
Ebbinghaus/Preissler,
Ermordung, testimony by N.N.
Akinowa on 18.11.46, lengthy
quotation, ibid., p.88ff. In addi-
tion, see statement by Georg
Frentzel, 27.8.70, and Alexander
N. Stepanow (then Director of
the psychiatric hospital in
Mogilew), 20.7.44, both in StA
Munich, Zentraler
Untersuchungsvorgang 9.

6 Beer, *Entwicklung*, p.409ff.; in
addition, see statement by
Widmann in ZSt, 202 AR-Z
152/59, p.33ff., 11.1.60.

7 Beer, *Entwicklung*, p.411.

8 Even before Christmas 1941
more vehicles were driven from
Berlin to Riga to EG A. See

Beer, *Entwicklung*, p. 413. For
SK 4a (EG C), see Beer,
Entwicklung, p.412. For EK 8
(EG B), see the statement by
Otto Matonoga, 8.6/9.6.45 to
the Soviet investigators (StA
Munich, Zentraler
Untersuchungsvorgang 9).
According to the testimony of
one witness, EG D used a gas
van at the end of 1941: see
Beer, *Entwicklung*, p. 413; LG
München, 119 c Js 1/69,
Judgement; statement by
Jeckeln of 21.12.45 (published
in Wilhelm, *Einsatzgruppe*
A/Truppe, p.548).

9 *Nationalsozialistische
Massentötungen*, p.110ff.

10 Pressac, *Krematorien*, p.41f.;
Czech, *Kalendarium*, p.115ff.;
Brandhuber, *Kriegsgefangene* and
Barcz, *Die erste Vergasung*, in
Adler et al., *Auschwitz*, p.17f..

11 *Commandant*, p.144ff.

12 Ibid., p.183.

13 Pressac, *Krematorien*, pp.38ff.

14 See Aly, *Final Solution*, p.323ff..

15 Gerlach, *Failure*.

16 In this context, see Hitler's state-
ments in the conversation about
'Eastern questions' on 16 July
(*IMT*, XXXVIII, p.86ff., 221-L).

17 Kershaw, *Final Solution*, p.65. In
1942 information to the effect
that the Jews of the District of
Konin, 3,000 people in all, had
been systematically murdered got
through to the United States. This
was confirmed by a German
investigative proceeding (see ZSt,

206 AR–Z 228/73).

18 Judgement, LG Stuttgart,
15.8.50, published in *Justiz*,VII,
231a.

19 Aly, *Final Solution*, p.70ff.

20 PRO, HW 16/32, 4.10.41.

21 Statement of Lange's driver,
Justiz, XXI, no. 594, LG Bonn,
Judgement, 23.7.65;
*Nationalsozialistische-
Massentötungen*, p.110ff.

22 *Faschismus*, p.278.

23 The report of the Gestapo in
Lodz ('*Judentum*') also points to
the central role of Greiser: see
Faschismus, p.285.

24 *Diensttagebuch*, 14.10.41.

25 Ibid., esp. p.427f.The regulation
was back-dated to 15.10.
Published in, *Faschismus*, p.128f.

26 IfZ, MA 120, in brief in
Diensttagebuch, p.436.

27 IfZ, MA 120, in brief in
Diensttagebuch, p.436.

28 Pohl, *Ostgalizien*, p.140ff.The
abbreviation 'z.b.V.' means '*zur
besonderen Verwendung*', for special
purposes.The unit consisted of
members of the Security Police
in the Generalgouvernement
Poland and was deployed in this
area.Typical of this phase is, for
example, the 'Intelligence-
Action' in Stanislau on 3 August
in which 600 men were shot
(Judgement LG Münster,
31.5.1968, 5 Ks 4/65, IfZ, Gm
08.08).

29 Pohl, *Ostgalizien*, p.138.

30 IfZ, Gm 08.08, Judgement LG
Münster, 31.5.68, 5 Ks 4/65,

statement by the Head of the
outpost Krüger, vol. 30, p.96f.

31 On Stanislau, see Pohl,
Ostgalizien, p.144ff.

32 *Dienstkalender*.

33 BAB, BDC-File Globocnik,
Letter to Himmler of 1.10.1941.
Cf. Pohl, *Lublin*, p.101.

34 ZSt, 208 AR–Z 252/59, vol. 6,
p.1179, statement of Stanislaw
Kozak. Start of construction
was 1.11.41. Published in *NS-
Massentötungen*, p.152f.
Tregenza's study, *Belzec*, con-
firms this date.

35 According to Arad, *Belzec*, p.17,
the first group of the
'Euthanasia' personnel arrived
in Belzec between the end of
October and the end of
December.

36 Pohl, *Lublin*, pp. 101 and 105f.

37 Manoschek, *Serbien*, p.43f.

38 Ibid., p.49ff.

39 Ibid., p.79ff.The order originally mentioned 2,100 victims,
but the figure was raised by 100
after another German soldier
died.

40 Ibid., p.86ff.

41 NG 3354; Manoschek, *Serbien*,
p.104

42 NG 3354; Manoschek, *Serbien*,
p.102.

43 Ibid., p.84f.

44 Ibid., p.96f.

45 Ibid. p.86.

46 PAA, Inland IIg 104, Bericht
Rademacher 7.11.41;
Manoschek, *Serbien*, p 102ff.

47 Longerich, *Politik*, p.460.

48 Safrian, *Eichmann-Männer*,
p.153f.

49 'Deportatoion of Jews from
Berlin – no liquidation'
(*Dienstkalender*). Although the
order only referred concretely to
the transport from Berlin, it led
to a temporary halt being called
to the liquidations of Jews from
the area of the Greater German
Reich in the Baltic States. The
mere fact that Himmler was in
the extensive area of the Führer's
headquarters during his telephone call of 30 November does
not permit the conclusion that
the order came from Hitler. In
fact, it was only after the telephone call that the two were to
meet and discuss the matter at
length (*Dienstkalender*).

50 *Dienstkalender*, 30.11., 1.12. u.
4.12.41 and PRO, HW 16/32,
1.12. u. 4.12.

51 See p.130.

52 Draft of the speech quoted in
Wilhelm, *Rassenpolitik*, p.131
from PAA, Pol XIII, 25, VAA-
Reports: draft.). See also the
notes of a reporter ('strictly
confidential informational
report') from this press conference: 'The number of Jews in
this entire area is estimated at 6
million, brought across the
Urals in the course of the year
or otherwise became somehow
victim to extermination':
Hagemann, *Presselenkung*, p.146.

CHAPTER 15

1 *Tagebücher Goebbels*, 13.12.41.
2 See p.148f.
3 PS-1517, *IMT*, XXVII, p.270ff.
4 *Dienstkalender*.
5 Neither this note nor Hitler's
statements on 12 December can
be adduced as proof of a 'basic
decision' on Hitler's part to
carry out the murder of all
European Jews in the context of
the declaration of war against
the USA, as does Gerlach,
Wannsee-Konferenz (on this see
Longerich, *Politik*, p.466ff.).
6 *Domarus*, II, 1821.
7 Ibid., II, p.1828f.
8 *Völkischer Beobachter*, 26.2.42,
published in Domarus, II, 1844.
9 *Monologe*, 27.1.42
10 Ibid., 22.2.42.
11 *Tagebücher Goebbels*, 15.2.42.

CHAPTER 16

1 PAA, Inland II g, 177, no. 16,
published in *Ermordung*
(Longerich), p.83ff.
2 On the forced labour complex
at this period, see Longerich,
Politik, p.476 ff.
3 *Diensttagebuch*, p.457f.
4 *Diensttagebuch*, 16.12.1941.

CHAPTER 17

1 1063-PS, published in
Ermordung (Longerich), pp.165f.

See also the 'Guidelines for the technical implementation of the evacuations of Jews from the Genralgouvernement' (*Richtlinien zur technischen Durchführung der Evakuierung von Juden in das Generalgouvernement*), IfZ, Collection of Edicts of the Gestapo Würzburg, published in Adler, *Mensch*, p.191f.

2 Transcript of a meeting on 9.3.43, Eichmann Trial, doc. 119, published in *Ermordung* (Longerich), p.167ff.

3 Note by Reuter, Department for Population and Welfare (*Abteilung Bevölkerungswesen und Fürsorge*), 17.3.11942, quoted from Adler, *Theresienstadt*, pp.50f.

4 See Longerich, *Politik*, p.484ff.

5 Ibid., p.492.

6 Klarsfeld, *Vichy*, p.43.

7 Note by Dannecker, 10.3.41, 1216-RF, published in Klarsfeld, *Vichy*, p.374f.

8 Record by Zeitschel, 11.3.42, published in Klarsfeld, *Vichy*, p.375.

9 Klarsfeld, *Vichy*, p.34ff.

10 Moreshet-Archive, Givat Haviva, Israel (copy from the Prague State Archive, 114-7-300), published in *Tragedia Slovenskych Zidov. Fotografie a Dokumenty*, Bratislava 1949.

11 Note by Dannecker 15.6., RF 1217, published in Klarsfeld, *Vichy*, p.379ff.; cf. Klarsfeld's

intrepretation, ibid., p.66f.

12 Pohl, *Lublin*, p.109ff.; Lvov State Archive, R 37 (Stadthauptmann Lemberg), 4-140, note in file of 10.1.1940 concerning the meeting of the administration of the district (copy in the USHMM Washington); Pohl, *Ostgalizien*, p.180ff.

13 Safrian, *Eichman-Männer*, pp.150ff.

14 Fleming, *Hitler*, p.87ff.

15 *Dienstkalender*, 14.3.42.

16 Pohl, *Ostgalizien*, p.179ff.

17 Pohl, *Ostgalizien*, p.104.

18 *Tagebücher Goebbels*, 27.3.42.

19 Ibid., 20.3.1942.

20 Manoschek, *Serbien*, p.169ff.

CHAPTER 18

1 VOGG, 1942, p.321ff., 'Instruction Concerning the Transfer of Duties to the State Secretary for Security (*Erlaß über die Überweisung von Dienstgeschäften auf den Staatssekretär für das Sicherheitswesen*); cf. Pohl, *Lublin*, p.125.

2 Arad, *Belzec*, p.37ff.

3 Pohl, *Lublin*, p.120ff.

4 Pohl, *Lublin*, p.122; Pohl, *Ostgalizien*, p.195.

5 *Diensttagebuch*.

6 Arad, *Belzec*, pp.126f., 383ff.

7 Ibid., p.393ff.

8 Steinbacher, *Auschwitz*, p.278ff.

9 Details in Longerich, *Politik*, p.490.

10 Judgement LG Koblenz 21.5.63, published in *Justiz* XIX, no. 552 (Heuser case). On the shootings, see also the Activity Reports of the II. Platoon, Waffen-SS Btl. z.b.V., published in *Unsere Ehre*, p.236ff.

11 Details in Longerich, *Politik*, p.490.

12 Büchler, *Deportation*.

13 Witte, *Decisions*, p.335f.

14 Longerich, *Politik*, p.511ff.; Pohl, *Ukraine*; Gerlach, *Morde*, p.683ff.

15 Czech, *Kalendarium*.

16 Longerich, *Politik*, p.508.

17 BAB, NS 19/1757, published in *Ermordung*,(Longerich), p.201.

18 BAB, NS 19/2655, Ganzenmüller to Wolff on 29.7.1941.

19 It is not clear from Himmler's notes what was discussed at these meetings. The only exception is his report to Hitler on 3 May: from the notes by Himmler that have been preserved, it emerges that the topic was matters relating to the Waffen-SS; but other, non-military subjects were also discussed, which Himmler did not record (*Dienstkalender*, p.415, note 6).

20 Schmidt-Hartmann, *Tschechoslowakei*, p.362.

21 Himmler, *Geheimreden*, p.159.

22 See esp. chs 11; 13, 14, 15, 17, 20, 21.

23 *Tagebücher Goebbels*, 27.4.42.

24 See p.173.

25 The fact that there was a language-regulation within the National Socialist system, according to which mass murder of Jews was to be described as 'resettlement', can be shown in many instances. For example, the command post of Bachtsschissaray, a unit-station of the Wehrmacht in the occupied Soviet Union noted in its activity report of 14.12.1941 the murder of the Jews living in that area: 'The Jews who had been residing here were not rich and lived in a relatively modest manner. The S.D. carried out the shooting of the Jews on 13.12.1941.' In the report, the word 'shooting' (*Erschießung*) was crossed out by hand and replaced by the word 'resettlement' (*Aussiedlung*) (Zst Dok. USA, 29). The commander of the Security Police and the SD in White Ruthenia issued an instruction on 5.2.1943 in which he ordered the 'resettlement' of the Jews living in the city of Sluzk. The order continues, 'in the resettlement site there are two ditches. Each ditch is worked on by a group of ten leaders and men, relieved every two hours.' The order also determined who was to be responsible for 'distributing cartridges' on the 'resettlement site' (ZSt, Dok. USSR, 107). Himmler used the word 'resettlement' (*Umsiedlung*) in a

document from July 1942, for example, to order the murder of the large majority of the Jews in the Generalgouvernement Poland by the end of that year (see footnote 17).

26 The so-called 'Schlegelberger Note' can be used in support of this argument only with very strong reservations (BAB, R 22/52). In a note located in the records of the Reichsjustizministerium, a civil servant in this ministry, possibly Secretary of State Franz Schlegelberger himself, noted that Lammers the Head of the Reichskanzlei, had informed him that the Führer had 'repeatedly informed him [Lammers] that he wished it to be clear that the solution to the Jewish question had been postponed until after the war. In accordance with this, in the opinion of Reichsminister Lammers, the current discussions have only a theoretical value. He is however concerned above all to prevent fundamental decisions being taken without his knowledge on the basis of a surprise report from another quarter.' The note is undated and unsigned. The date and authorship cannot be established with anything approaching certainty. This document conveys the information that Lammers's was *supposed* to

have at that point, but it does not say when Lammers received this information from Hitler. If the document is dated before the Wannsee Conference (20 January 1942), the information that Hitler wanted to postpone the 'solution to the Jewish question' until after the war is of no particular importance. If it is of a later date, and if one assumes that it contains accurately the information *currently* possessed by Lammers, then there is reason to think that the formulation 'solution to the Jewish question' refers to the problem of 'mixed-raced Jews' that had not been decided even after the Wannsee Conference, and which was the object of discussion between the relevant ministries (including the Justice Ministry). However, if one assumes that the document was written in spring 1942, and that the formulation 'solution to the Jewish question' indeed refers to the 'Jewish question' as a whole, and if one supposes that Schlegelberger was reporting Lammers correctly and that Lammers was reporting Hitler correctly, then this document can only be interpreted in the same way as Hitler's remarks to Goebbels in April and May – as an expression of Hitler's conception that the murders that had already been carried out of hundreds of thousands of people in

Eastern Europe did not yet represent the real 'final solution', and that this would take place at a later date and only be completed after the end of the war.

27 Picker, *Tischgespräche*.
28 Information from Rademacher to Bielfeld, 10.2.42, published in Brechtken, *Madagaskar*, p.279.

CHAPTER 19

1 *Tagebücher Goebbels* 30.5.42.
2 *Deutschlands Rüstung*, 20-22.9.42, p.189.
3 *Tagebücher Goebbels*, 30.9.42.
4 Domarus, II, pp.1913ff, 1920. Hitler repeated this threat in another speech on 8 November 1942 (ibid., pp.1933ff, 1937).
5 See footnote 2.
6 No. 1611; published in facsimile in Grabitz/Scheffler, *Spuren*, p.179.
7 BAB, NS 19/291.
8 Hilberg, *Vernichtung*, p.761
9 Rautkallio, *Finland*, p.82f.
10 Browning, *Solution*, p.115ff.; for the exchange of documents on this topic, see PAA, Inland IIg 200.
11 PAA, Inland IIg 177, Ribbentrop to Luther, 25.8.42.
12 Ibid., note by Luther, 21.8.42.; Inland IIg 208, letter from Eichmann to the Foreign Ministry, 25.9.42.
13 PAA, Inland IIg 183, speech note by Luther, 10.9.1942;

Chary, *Bulgaria*,pp.113ff.; Browning, *Solution*, p.123.
14 PAA, Inland IIg 177, speech note by Luther,11.9.42; Carpi, *Rescue*, p.717.
15 PAA, Inland IIg 190, Suhr to Rademacher, 11.7.42; Carpi, *Notes*, p.738ff.
16 PAA, Inland II g 208, note by Luther for von Weizsäcker v. 24.9.42.
17 See p.191.
18 *Staatsmänner* II, p.111ff., note of 25.9 on the discussion of 24.9, p.118f.
19 *Staatsmänner* II, p.106ff. on the conversation between Hitler and Antonescu, and PAA, Inland II g 200, report by Richter, 26.11.42 on Antonescu's remarks and his separate conversation Ribbentrop. See also Browning, *Solution*, p.124f.
20 See p.188f.
21 Details in Longerich, *Politik*, p.528ff., based on the documents of the PAA, Inland IIg 200 (Rumania), IIg 183 (Bulgaria), and IIg 208 (Hungary). On Slovakia, see Lipscher, *Juden*, p.129ff..
22 PAA, Inland IIg 194; Browning, *Solution*, p.137ff.
23 Herbert, *Best*, p.330ff.
24 Abrahamsen, *Response*, p.94ff.

CHAPTER 20

1 Pohl, *Ostgalizien*, p.248ff.; Arad, *Belzec*, p.127 and 392ff.

2 No. 1882, Himmler to Krüger, January 1943.
3 See p.188.
4 Adler, *Mensch*, pp.224ff.
5 Fleischer, *Griechenland*, p.273.
6 Chary, *Bulgaria*, pp.129ff and 197ff.
7 Abitol, *Juifs*.
8 *Dienstkalender*.
9 BAB, Slg. Schumacher, no. 484.
10 Vichy, *Klarsfeld*, p.193ff.; Zuccotti, *Holocaust*, p.166ff.
11 *Dienstkalender*; BAB, NS 19/159.
12 Dienstkalender; see also Wenck, *Menschenhandel*, p.76ff. and Bauer, *Jews*, p.103ff.
13 *Tagebücher Goebbels*, 25.4.43; BAB, NS 19/2648, Himmler to Greifelt, 12.5.43.
14 *Diensttagebuch*, 31.5.1943.
15 Steinbacher, *Auschwitz*, p.295ff.
16 CDJC, XXVII-17, memo by Hagen, 16.6.43, published in Klarsfeld, *Vichy*, p.535.
17 Hirschfeld, *Niederlande*, p.162ff.

18 PAA, Inland IIg 194; Hilberg, *Vernichtung*, p.764.
19 Lipscher, *Juden*, pp.146 and 150.
20 BAB, NS 19/1432.
21 Longerich, *Politik*, p.555f.
22 *IMT*, XXXV, p.426ff., D-736.
23 See the account in Braham, *Politics*.
24 Lipscher, *Juden*, p.178f.

CHAPTER 21

1 Himmler, *Geheimreden*, p.169.
2 IfZ, MA 314, pp.3449ff., 3476ff.
3 IfZ, MA 316, pp.4609ff., 4639f.; published in Himmler, *Geheimreden*, p.203.
4 IfZ, MA 315, pp.3945ff., 3961.
5 IfZ, MA 316, pp.4971ff., 5021; see also Wilhelm, *Hitlers Ansprache*.
6 Streicher-9, *IMT*, XLI, pp.549ff.

BIBLIOGRAPHY

PRIMARY SOURCES

BUNDESARCHIV BERLIN

BDC	Former Berlin Document Centre
NS 19	Reichsführer SS
NS 33	SS-Führungshauptamt
NS 36	Oberstes Parteigericht der NSDAP
R 2	Reichsfinanzministerium
R 6	Ostministerium
R 20	Ordnungspolizei
R 22	Reichsjustizministerium.
R 43 II	Reichskanzlei
R 58.	Gestapo
R 70	Police forces in the occupied territories
25-01	Reichsbank

BUNDESARCHIV/MILITÄRARCHIV FREIBURG

RH 20	Armeen
RW 4	Wehrmachtführungsstab
RW 19	Wirtschafts- und Rüstungsamt

POLITISCHES ARCHIV DES AUSWÄRTIGEN AMTES BERLIN

Inland IIg
Pol Abt.

INSTITUT FÜR ZEITGESCHICHTE MUNICH

Fb	Photocopies
G	Trials
MA	Microfilms

Partei-Kanzlei der NSDAP, Rundschreiben
Nuremberg Documents (NG und NO series)

STAATSANWALTSCHAFT MUNICH
Verfahrensakten
Zentraler Untersuchungsvorgang 9

                    STAATSARCHIV WOLFENBÜTTEL
62 Nds   NS-Verfahren

                    ZENTRALE STELLE LUDWIGSBURG
Verfahrensakten
Dokumentation
Anklagen
Urteile

    CENTRE DE DOCUMENTATION JUIVE CONTEMPORAINE PARIS
Files regarding German occupation of France (available as photocopies in
    Yad Vashem)

                    OSOBI ARCHIVE MOSKAU
Fonds 500   RSHA

                    PUBLIC RECORD OFFICE LONDON
HW 16   \ Deciphered German documents

                    STATE ARCHIVE MINSK
Fonds 655   German civil administration (available as photo
                    copies in US Holocaust Museum)

                    STATE ARCHIVE LVOV
R 37   Stadthauptmann Lemberg (available as photocopies
                    in US Holocaust Museum Washington .

                    STATE ARCHIVE PRAGUE (SUA)
No. 114   Reichsprotektor (available as photocopies in Yad
                    Vashem and in Moreshet Archive Givat Haviva)

                    YAD VASHEM ARCHIVES JERUSALEM
YV 053   German Police Units .
JM   Microfilms

PUBLISHED DOCUMENTS

Akten zur Deutschen Auswärtigen Politik, Series C: 1933-1937, 6 vols (Göttingen 1971-1982); Series D: 1937-1941, 13 vols (Baden-Baden u. Göttingen 1950-1970); Series E: 1941-1945, 8 vols (Göttingen 1969-1979)

Akten der Reichskanzlei. Die Regierung Hitler, Teil I 1933/34, 2 vols, (Boppard a. Rh. 1983)

Aly, Götz, and Susanne Heim, 'Staatliche Ordnung und organische Lösung. Die Rede Hermann Görings, über die Judenfrage, vom 6, Dezember 1938', in *Jahrbuch für Antisemitismusforschung 2* (1993) pp.378-404

'Aus dem Kriegstagebuch des Diplomaten Otto Bräutigam'H.D. Heilmann (ed.), in *Biedermann und Schreibtischtäter: Materialien zur deutschen Täter-Biographie*, Götz Aly et al. (eds) (Berlin 1987)

Auschwitz. Zeugnisse und Berichte, H. G. Adler, Hermann Langbein and Ella Lingens-Reiner (eds), 2nd edn (Cologne 1972)

Below, Nicolaus von, *Als Hitlers Adjutant, 1937-45* (Mainz 1980)

Commandant of Auschwitz:The Autobiography of Rudolf Hoess (London 1959)

Ciano's Diplomatic Papers, Malcolm Muggeridge (ed.) (London 1948)

Ciano, Galleazzo, *Tagebücher 1939-1943* (Hamburg 1949)

Denkschrift Himmlers über die Behandlung der Fremdvölkischen im Osten (Mai 1940), Helmut Krausnick (ed.) in *VfZ 5* (1957), pp.194-198

Deutschlands Rüstung im Zweiten Weltkrieg. Hitlers Konferenzen mit Albert Speer 1942-1945, Willi A. Boelcke (ed.) (Frankfurt a. M. 1969)

Der Dienstkalender Heinrich Himmlers 1941/42, Peter Witte et al. (eds) (Hamburg 1999)

Das Diensttagebuch des deutschen Generalgouverneurs in Polen 1939-1945, Ernst Präg and Wolfgang Jacobmeyer (eds) (Stuttgart 1975)

Dokumente über die Verfolgung der jüdischen Bürger in Baden-Württemberg durch das nationalsozialistische Regime, Paul Sauer (ed.) 2 vols (Stuttgart 1966)

Dokumenty i Materialy do Dziejów okupacji niemieckiej w Polsce, 3 vols (Warszawa, Lodz, Kraków 1946)

Domarus, Max, *Hitler. Reden und Proklamationen*, 2 vols (Würzburg 1963)

Die Einsatzgruppen in der besetzten Sowjetunion 1941/42. Die Tätigkeits- und Lageberichte des Chefs der Sicherheitspolizei und des SD, Peter Klein (ed.) (Berlin 1997)

Die Endlösung der Judenfrage in Belgien. Deutsche Dokumente 1941-1944, Serge Klarsfeld (ed.) (Cologne 1977)

Die Ermordung der europäischen Juden. Eine umfassende Dokumentation des Holocaust 1941-1945, Peter Longerich (ed.) (Munich 1989)

'Die Ermordung psychisch kranker Menschen in der Sowjetunion.
    Dokumentation', compiled by Angelika Ebbinghaus and Gerd Preissler
    in *Aussonderung und Tod. Die klinische Hinrichtung der Unbrauchbaren*,
    Götz Aly (ed.) (Berlin 1985), pp.9-74
*Faschismus – Getto – Massenmord. Dokumentation über Ausrottung und
    Widerstand der Juden in Polen während des zweiten Weltkrieges* (Frankfurt
    a. M. 1962)
Die faschistische Okkupationspolitik in Polen 1939-1945, Werner Röhr (ed.)
    (Cologne 1988)
Grabitz, Helge, and Wolfgang Scheffler, *Letzte Spuren. Ghetto Warschau,
    SS-Arbeitslager Trawniki, Aktion Erntefest, Fotos und Dokumente über
    Opfer des Endlösungswahns im Spiegel der historischen Ereignisse* (Berlin
    1988)
Groscurth, Helmuth, *Tagebücher eines Abwehroffiziers 1938-1940. Mit weiteren
    Dokumenten zur Militäropposition gegen Hitler*, Helmut Krausnick and
    Harold C. Deutsch (eds) (Stuttgart 1970)
Halder, Franz, *Kriegstagebuch. Tägliche Aufzeichnungen des Chefs des
    Generalstabs des Heeres 1939-1942*, Walther Hubatsch (ed.) 2nd edn
    (Koblenz 1983)
Himmler, Heinrich, *Geheimreden 1933 bis 1945 und andere Ansprachen*, Bradley
    Smith and Agnes F. Peterson (eds) (Frankfurt a. M., Berlin, Wien 1974)
Hitler, Adolf, *Mein Kampf* (Munich 1941)
Hitler. Reden, Schriften, Anordnungen, part I-VI (Munich etc. 1992-1998)
Hitler. Sämtliche Aufzeichnungen 1905-1924. Eberhard Jäckel and Axel Kuhn
    (eds) (Stuttgart 1980)
'Hitlers Denkschrift zum Vierjahresplan 1936', Wilhelm Treue (ed.) in
    VfZ 3 (1955), pp.184-203
*Hitlers Weisungen für die Kriegführung 1939-1945. Dokumente des Oberkommandos
    der Wehrmacht*, Walther Hubatsch (ed.), 2nd edn (Koblenz 1983)
Hoche, Alfred and Karl Binding, *Die Freigabe der Vernichtung lebensunwerten
    Lebens. Ihr Maß und ihre Form* (Leipzig 1920)
Jordan, Rudolf, *Erlebt und Erlitten. Weg eines Gauleiters von München bis
    Moskau* (Leoni am Starnberger See 1971)
*Justiz und NS-Verbrechen. Sammlung deutscher Strafurteile wegen national-
    sozialistischer Tötungsverbrechen*, Irene Sagel-Grande, Adelheid Rüther-
    Elemann and C.F. Rüter (eds), 22 vols (Amsterdam 1968-1981)
*Das Kriegstagebuch des Oberkommandos der Wehrmacht
    (Wehrmachtführungsstab), 1940-1945*, Percy Ernst Schramm (ed.), 4 vols
    (Frankfurt a. M. 1961-1979)
Kropat, Wolf-Arno, *Kristallnacht in Hessen. Der Judenpogrom vom November
    1938. Eine Dokumentation* (Wiesbaden 1988)

Lagevorträge des Oberbefehlshabers der Kriegsmarine vor Hitler 1939-1945,
  Gerhard Wagner (ed.) (Munich 1972)
Monologe im Führerhauptquartier. Die Aufzeichnungen Heinrich Heims,
  Jochmann (ed.) (Hamburg 1980)
Nationalsozialistische Massentötungen durch Giftgas. Eine Dokumentation,
  Eugen Kogon et al. (eds) (Frankfurt a. M. 1983)
*Parteitag der Freiheit. Reden des Führers und ausgewählte Kongreßreden am
  Reichsparteitag der NSDAP* (Munich 1935)
Picker, Henry, *Hitlers Tischgespräche im* Führer*hauptquartier 1941-1942*, Percy
  Ernst Schramm (ed.) (Stuttgart 1963)
Das politische Tagebuch Alfred Rosenbergs aus den Jahren 1934/35 und 1939/40,
  Hans-Günther Seraphim (ed.) (Göttingen 1956)
Protektoratny Kárny and Milotová Miroslav and Kárná Jaroslava and
  Margita (eds) *Protektorátní politika Reinharda Heydricha* (Prague 1991)
Reichsgesetzblatt (Berlin)
Reichsministerialblatt für die innere Verwaltung (Berlin)
'Das Reichsministerium des Innern und die Judengesetzgebung.
  Aufzeichnungen von Dr Bernhard Lösener', Walter Strauss (ed.) in *VfZ*
  9 (1961), pp.262-313
Reichstagung in Nürnberg 1937. Der Parteitag der Arbeit, Hans Kerrl (ed.)
  (Berlin 1937)
Schirach, Baldur von, *Ich glaubte an Hitler* (Hamburg 1967)
Schirach, Henriette von, *Der Preis der Herrlichkeit. Erlebte Zeitgeschichte*
  (Munich/Berlin 1956)
Schmidt, Paul, *Statist auf politischer Bühne 1923-1945. Erlebnisse des
  Chefdolmetschers im Auswärtigen Amt mit den Staatsmännern Europas*
  (Bonn 1953)
Die Schoah von Babi Yar, Roy Wiehn (ed.) (Konstanz 1991)
*Das Sonderrecht für Juden im NS-Staat. Eine Sammlung der gesetzlichen
  Maßnahmen und Richtlinien – Inhalt und Bedeutung*, Joseph Walk (ed.)
  (Heidelberg 1981)
*Staatsmänner und Diplomaten bei Hitler. Vertrauliche Aufzeichnungen über
  Unterredungen mit Vertretern des Auslandes 1939-1941*, Andreas Hillbruber
  (ed.), 2 vols (Frankfurt a. M. 1967)
*Die Tagebücher von Joseph Goebbels. Sämtliche Fragmente, Teil 1:
  Aufzeichnungen 1923-1941*, Elke Fröhlich (ed.), 4 vols (Munich 1987)
Die Tagebücher von Joseph Goebbels, Teil 1: Aufzeichnungen 1923-1941, Elke
  Fröhlich (ed.), vols 6-9 (Munich 1998)
Die Tagebücher von Joseph Goebbels. Teil 2: Diktate 1941-1945, Elke Fröhlich
  (ed.), 15 vols (Munich 1994-1996)

'Those were the days': The Holocaust through the Eyes of the Perpetrators and
    Bystanders, Ernst Klee, Willi Dressen and Volker Riess (eds) (London
    1991)
Tory, Avraham, Surviving the Holocaust. The Kovno Ghetto Diary
    (Cambridge, Mass./London 1990)
The Trial of Adolf Eichmann, 9 vols (Jerusalem 1992-1995)
The Trial of the Major War Criminals Before the International Military Tribunal
    at Nuremberg, International Military Tribunal, 14.10.45-1.10.46, 42 vols
    (1947-1949)
Unsere Ehre heißt Treue. Kriegstagebuch des Kommandostabes Reichsführer SS.
    Tätigkeitsberichte der 1. u. 2. SS-Inf.-Brigade, der 1. SS-Kav.-Brigade und
    von Sonderkommandos der SS (Vienna, Munich, Zurich 1965)
Verhandlungen des Reichstages (Berlin)
Verfolgung, Vertreibung, Vernichtung: Dokumente des faschistischen Antisemitismus
    1933 bis 1942, Kurt Pätzold (ed.) (Frankfurt a. M. 1984)
Verordnungsblatt des Generalgouvernements
Völkischer Beobachter (Munich)
Wilhelm, Hans-Heinrich, Rassenpolitik und Kriegführung. Sicherheitspolizei
    und Wehrmacht in Polen und der Sowjetunion (Passau 1991)

                          SECONDARY LITERATURE

Abitol, Michel, Les Juifs d'Afrique du Nord sous Vichy (Paris 1983)
Abrahamsen, Samuel, Norway's Response to the Holocaust (New York 1991)
Adam, Uwe, Judenpolitik im Dritten Reich (Düsseldorf 1972)
Adler, Hans-Günther, Theresienstadt 1941-1945. Das Antlitz einer
    Zwangsgemeinschaft, Geschichte, Soziologie, Psychologie, 2nd edn (Tübingen 1960)
Adler, Hans-Günther, Der verwaltete Mensch: Studien zur Deportation der
    Juden aus Deutschland (Tübingen 1974)
Aly, Götz, and Susanne Heim, Vordenker der Vernichtung. Auschwitz und die
    deutschen Pläne für eine neue europäische Ordnung (Hamburg 1991)
Aly, Götz, 'Final Solution': Nazi Population Policy & the Murder of the
    European Jews (London 1999)
Angrick, Andrej, and Martina Vogt, and Silke Ammerschubert and Peter
    Klein, "'Da hätte man schon ein Tagebuch führen müssen". Das
    Polizeibataillon 322 und die Judenmorde im Bereich der Heesgruppe Mitte
    wärend des Sommers und Herbstes 1941', in: Die Normalität des Verbrechens,
    Helge Grabitz and Klaus Bästlein and Johannes Tuchel (eds) (Berlin 1994),
    pp. 325-385

Arad, Yitzhak, *Belzec, Sobibor, Treblinka: the Operation Reinhard death camps* (Bloomington 1987)

—, *Ghetto in flames: the struggle and destruction of the Jews in Vilna in the Holocaust* (Jerusalem/New York 1981)

Arndt, Ino, and Heinz Boberach, 'Deutsches Reich', in: *Dimension des Völkermords*, pp.3-65

Barkai, Avraham, *Vom Boykott zu 'Endjudung'. Der wirtschaftliche Existenzkampf der Juden im Dritten Reich 1933-1943* (Frankfurt a. M. 1988)

Bauer, Yehuda, *Jews For Sale? Nazi-Jewish Negotiations, 1933-1945* (New Haven 1994)

Beer, Matthias, 'Die Entwickung der Gaswagen beim Mord an den Juden', in *VfZ 35* (1987), pp.403-417

Benz, Wolfgang, 'Der Rückfall in die Barbarei, Bericht über den Pogrom', in *Der Judenpogrom 1938. Von der 'Reichskristallnacht' zum Völkermord*, Walter H. Pehle (ed.) (Frankfurt/M. 1988) pp.13-51

Bernhardt, Heike, 'Anstaltspsychiatrie und "Euthanasie"' in *Pommern 1939-1945. Die Krankenmorde an Kindern und Erwachsenen am Beispiel der Landesheilanstalt Ueckermünde* (Frankfurt a. M. 1994)

Boog, Horst et. al., *Der Angriff auf die Sowjetunion* (Stuttgart 1983)

Botz, Gerhard, 'Wohnungpolitik und Judendeportation', in *Wien 1938 bis 1945. Zur Funktion des Antisemitismus als Ersatz nationalsozialistischer Sozialpolitik* (Vienna, Salzburg 1975)

Braham, Randolph L., *The Politics of Genocide*, 2 vols (New York 1981)

Brandhuber, Jerzy, 'Die sowjetischen Kriegsgefangenen im Konzentrationslager Auschwitz', in *Hefte von Auschwitz 4* (1961), pp.5-46

Brechtken, Magnus, *'Madagaskar für die Juden'. Antisemitische Idee und politische Praxis 1885-1945* (Munich 1997)

Breitman, Richard, *The Architect of Genocide: Himmler and the Final Solution* (London 1991)

Broszat, Martin, *Nationalsozialistische Polenpolitik* (Stuttgart 1961)

Broszat, Martin, 'Hitler and the genesis of the 'final solution': An assessment of David Irving's theses', in *Yad Vashem Studies 13* (1979), pp.73-125

Browning, Christopher R., *Fateful Months. Essays on the Emergence of the Final Solution* (New York/London 1985)

—, *The Final Solution and the German Foreign Office: A Study of Referat D III of Abteilung Deutschland 1940-43* (New York/London 1978)

—, *Nazi Policy, Jewish Workers, German Killers* (Cambridge 2000)

—, *Ordinary Men: Reserve Police Battalion 101 and the Final Solution in Poland* (New York 1992)

—, *Der Weg zur 'Endlösung'. Entscheidungen und Täter* (Bonn 1998)

Büchler, Yehoshua, 'The Deportation of Slovakian Jews to the Lublin District of Poland in 1942', in *HGS 6* (1991), pp.151-166

Burleigh, Michael, *Death and Deliverance: 'Euthanasia' in Germany, c.1900-1945* (Cambridge 1994)

Burrin, Philippe, *Hitler and the Jews* (London 1992)

Carpi, Daniel, 'Notes on the History of the Jews in Greece during the Holocaust Period. The Attitudes of the Italians (1941-1943)', in *Nazi Holocaust*, vol. 5, pp.731-768

Chary, Frederick Barry, *Bulgaria and the Jews: 'The Final Solution', 1940 to 1944* (PhD, University of Pittsburgh 1968)

Czech, Danuta, *Kalendarium der Ereignisse im Konzentrationslager Auschwitz-Birkenau 1939-1945* (Reinbek bei. Hamburg 1989)

Dimension des Völkermords: Die Zahl der jüdischen Opfer des Nationalsozialismus, Wolfgang Benz (ed.) (Munich 1991)

Dörner, Bernward, 'Justiz und Judenmord. Zur Unterdrückung von Äußerungen über den Genozid an den europäischen Juden durch die deutsche Justiz', in *Jahrbuch für Antisemitismus-Forschung* (1995), pp.226-253

Dröscher, Hans–Jürgen, *'Reichskristallnacht'. Die November-Pogrome 1938* (Frankfurt a. M./Berlin 1988)

Ezergailis, Andrew, *The Holocaust in Latvia 1941-1944: the Missing Center* (Riga/Washington 1996)

Faulstich, Heinz, *Hungersterben in der Psychiatrie 1914-1949. Mit einer Topographie der NS-Psychiatrie* (Freiburg i.B. 1998)

Fischer, Albert, *Hjalmar Schacht und Deutschlands 'Judenfrage'. Der 'Wirtschaftsdiktator' und die Vertreibung der Juden aus der Wirtschaft* (Cologne 1995)

Fleischer, Hagen, 'Griechenland', in *Dimension des Völkermords*, pp.241-274

Fleming, Gerald, *Hitler and the Final Solution* (Berkeley 1984)

Förster, Jürgen, 'Das andere Gesicht des Krieges: Das "Unternehmen Barbarossa" als Eroberungs- und Vernichtungskrieg', in *'Unternehmen Barbarossa'. Zum historischen Ort der deutsch-sowjetischen Beziehungen von 1933 bis Herbst 1941*, Roland G. Foerster (ed.) (Munich 1993), pp.151-162.

Friedlander, Henry, *The Origins of Nazi Genocide: From Euthanasia to the Final Solution* (Chapel Hill 1995)

Genschel, Helmut, *Die Verdrängung der Juden aus der Wirtschaft im Dritten Reich* (Berlin 1966)

Gerlach, Christian, 'Failure of Plans for an SS Extermination Camp in Mogilew, Belorussia', in *HGS 7* (1997), pp.60-78.

—, 'Deutsche Wirtschaftsinteressen, Besatzungspolitik und der Mord an den Juden in Weirußland, 1941-1943', in *Vernichtungspolitik*, Herbert (ed.), pp.263-291

—, 'Die Wannsee-Konferenz, das Schicksal der deutschen Juden und Hitlers politische Grundsatzentscheidung, alle Juden Europas zu ermorden', in *Werkstattgeschichte 18* (1997), pp.7-44

—, 'Kalkulieret Morde. Die deutsche Wirtschafts- und Vernichtungspolitik' in *Weißrußland 1941 bis 1944* (Hamburg 1999)

Gruchmann, Lothar, 'Justiz im Dritten Reich 1933-1940. Anpassung und Unterwerfung' in *der Ära Gürtner* (Munich 1988)

Hagemann, Jürgen, *Die Presselenkung im Dritten Reich* (Bonn 1970)

Hamann, Brigitte, *Hitler's Vienna. A dictator's apprenticeship* (New York/Oxford 1999)

Handbuch zur 'Völkischen Bewegung' 1871-1918, Uwe Puschner, Walter Schmitz n. Justus H. Ulbricht (ed.) (Munich 1996)

Headland, Ronald, *Messages of Murder: A Study of the Reports of the Einsatzgruppen of the Security Police and the Security Service, 1941-1943* (Rutherford, London 1992)

Held, Thomas, 'Vom Pogrom zum Massenmord. Die Vernichtung der jüdischen Bevölkerung Lembergs im Zweiten Weltkrieg', in Peter Fässler, Thomas Held, and Dirk Sawitzki (eds) *Lemberg – Lwów – Lviv* (Cologne/Weimar/Vienna 1993), pp.113-166

Herbert, Ulrich, *Best. Biographische Studien über Radikalismus, Weltanschauung und Vernunft, 1903-1989* (Bonn 1996)

—, 'Die deutsche Militärverwaltung in Paris und die Deportation der französischen Juden', in *Von der Aufgabe der Freiheit. Politische Verantwortung und bürgerliche Gesellschaft im 19. u. 20. Jahrhundert. Festschrift für Hans Mommsen zum 5. November 1995* Jansen, Christian Lutz Niethammer, Lutz, Weisbrod, Bernd (Berlin 1995), pp.427-450

Hilberg, Raul, *The Destruction of the European Jews* (New York/London 1985)

Hildebrand, Klaus, *The Third Reich* (London 1984)

Hirschfeld, Gerhard, 'Niederlande', in *Dimension des Völkermords*, pp.137-166

Jäckel, Eberhard, *Hitler's World View: A Blueprint for Power* (Cambridge, Mass 1972)

Jacobsen, Hans-Adolf, 'Kommissarbefehl und Massenexekutionen sowjetischer Kriegsgefangener', in *Anatomie des SS-Staats*, Buchheim et al. (eds), vol 2, 2nd edn (Munich 1979) pp.137-234

Jansen, Christian, and Arno Weckbecker, *Der 'Volksdeutsche Selbstschutz' in Polen 1939/40* (Munich 1992)

Joachimsthaler, Anton, *Hitlers Weg begann in München 1913-1923* (Munich 2000)

Kershaw, Ian, *Hitler* 2 vols (London 1998 and 2000)

—,'Improvised Genocide? The Emergence of the Final Solution in the Warthegau', in
    Transactions of the Royal Historical Society, 6th Series, 1992, pp.51-78
Kingreen, Monica, Jüdisches Landleben in Windecken, Ostheim und
    Heldenbergen (Hanau 1994)
Klarsfeld, Serge, Vichy – Auschwitz. Die Zusammenarbeit der deutschen und
    französischen Behörden bei der 'Endlösung der Judenfrage' in Frankreich
    (Nördlingen 1989)
Klee, Ernst, Euthanasie im NS-Staat. Die 'Vernichtung lebensunwerten Lebens'
    (Frankfurt a. M. 1983)
Krausnick, Helmut, and Hans-Heinrich Wilhelm, Die Truppe des
    Weltanschauungskrieges. Die Einsatzgruppen der Sicherheitspolizei und des
    SD 1938-1942 (Stuttgart l981)
—,'Die Einsatzgruppen vom Anschluß Österreichs bis zum Feldzug
    gegen die Sowjetunion. Entwicklung und Verhältnis zur Wehrmacht',
    in Krausnick, and Hans-Heinrich Wilhelm, Truppe, pp.13-278
—,'Judenverfolgung', in Hans Buchheim et. al., Anatomie des SS-Staates,
    vol. 2, 2nd edn (Munich 1979), pp.235-366
Lipscher, Ladislav, Die Juden im Slowakischen Staat, 1939-1945
    (Munich/Wien 1980)
Lipstadt, Deborah, Denying the Holocaust: The Growing Assault on Truth and
    Memory (New York 1993)
Lohalm, Uwe, Völkischer Radikalismus. Die Geschichte des Deutschvölkischen
    Schutz- und Trutzbundes, 1919-1923 (Hamburg 1970)
Longerich, Peter, 'Holocaust', in Handbook of Research on Violence, Wilhelm
    Heitmeyer, and John Hagen (eds) (Boulder 2002)
—,Politik der Vernichtung. Eine Gesamtdarstellung der nationalsozialistischen
    Judenverfolgung (Munich, Zurich 1998).
Majer, Diemut, 'Fremdvölkische' im Dritten Reich. Ein Beitrag zur national-
    sozialistischen Rechtssetzung und Rechtspraxis in Verwaltung und Justiz unter
    besonderer Berücksichtigung der eingegliederten Ostgebiete und des
    Generalgouvernements (Boppard a. Rh. 1981)
Manoschek, Walter, 'Serbien ist judenfrei'. Militärische Besatzungspolitik und
    Judenvernichtung in Serbien 1941/42 (Munich 1993)
Marrus, Michael/Paxton, Vichy France and the Jews (New York 1981)
Matzerath, Horst, 'Der Weg der Kölner Juden in den Holocaust. Versuch
    einer Rekonstruktion', in Die jüdischen Opfer des Nationalsozialismus aus
    Köln. Gedenkbuch (Cologne, Vienna 1995), pp.530-553
Mazower, Mark, Inside Hitler's Greece: The Experience of Occupation, 1941-
    1944 (New Haven/London 1993)
Moore, Bob, Victims and Survivors: The Nazi Persecution of the Jews in the
    Netherlands, 1940-1945 (London/New York 1997)

Moser, Jonny, 'Österreich', in *Dimension des Völkermords*, pp.67-93

Mosse, George L., *The Crisis of German Ideology: Intellectual Origins of the Third Reich* (New York 1964)

Müller, Rolf-Dieter, 'Von der Wirtschaftsallianz zum kolonialen Ausbeutungskrieg', in *Der Angriff auf die Sowjetunion*, Boog, Horst et al. (Stuttgart 1983), pp.141-245,

Musial, Bogdan, *Deutsche Zivilverwaltung und Judenverfolgung im Generalgouvernement* (Wiesbaden 1999)

—, '*Konterrevolutionäre Elemente sind zu erschießen'. Die Brutalisierung des deutsch-sowjetischen Krieges im Sommer 1941* (Berlin/Munich 2000)

Nationalsozialistische Vernichtungslager im Spiegel deutscher Strafprozesse. Belzec, Sobibor, Treblinka, Chelmno, Albert Rückerl (ed.) (Munich 1977)

National Socialist Extermination Policy. Contemporary German Perspectives and Controversies, Ulrich Herbert (ed.) (New York/Oxford 2000)

Obst, Dieter, '*Reichskristallnacht'. Ursachen und Verlauf des antisemitischen Pogroms vom November 1938* (Frankfurt a. M. etc. 1991)

Ogorreck, Ralf, *Die Einsatzgruppen und die 'Genesis der Endlösung'* (Berlin 1996)

Pätzold, Kurt, and Irene Runge, '*Kristallnacht'. Zum Pogrom 1938* (Cologne 1988)

Paul, Gerhard, *Aufstand der Bilder. Die NS-Propaganda vor 1933* (Bonn 1990)

Pelt, Robert-Jan van, and Deborah Dwork, *Auschwitz 1270 to the Present* (New Haven 1996)

Pohl, Dieter, *Von der 'Judenpolitik zum Judenmord'. Der Distrikt Lublin des Generalgouvernements 1939-1944* (Frankfurt a. M. etc. 1993)

Nationalsozialistische Judenverfolgung in Ostgalizien 1941-1944 (Munich 1996)

Popplow, Ullrich, 'Der Novemberpogrom 1938 in Minden und Göttingen', in *Göttinger Jahrbuch 28* (1980), pp.177-192

Pressac, Jean C., *Die Krematorien von Auschwitz. Die Technik des Massenmords* (Munich 1984)

Presser, Jacques, *The Destruction of the Dutch Jews* (New York 1969)

Rautkallio, Hannu, *Finland and the Holocaust: The Rescue of Finland's Jews* (New York 1987)

Reitlinger, Gerald, *The final solution: the attempt to exterminate the Jews of Europe, 1939-1945*, 2nd edn (South Brunswick 1968)

Rieß, Volker, *Die Anfänge der Vernichtung 'lebensunwerten Lebens' in den Reichsgauen Danzig-Westpreußen und Wartheland 1939/40* (Frankfurt a. M. etc. 1995)

Roth, Karl-Heinz, 'Heydrichs Professor. Historiographie des 'Volkstums' und der Massenvernichtungen: Der Fall Hans Joachim Beyer', in

Geschichtswissenschaft als Legitimationswissenschaft 1918-1945, Peter Schöttler (ed.) (Frankfurt. a. M. 1997), pp.262-316

Rüß, Hartmut, 'Wer war verantwortlich für das Massaker von Babij Jar?', in *MGM 57* (1998), pp.483-508

Safrian, Hans, *Die Eichmann-Männer* (Vienna 1993)

Sandkühler, Thomas, *Die 'Endlösung' in Galizien. Der Judenmord in Ostpolen und die Rettungsinitiative von Berthold Beitz 1941-1944* (Bonn 1996)

Schmidt-Hartmann, Eva, 'Tschechoslowakei', in *Dimension des Völkermords*, pp.353-380

Schmuhl, Walter, *Rassenhygiene, Nationalsozialismus, Euthanasie. Von der Verhütung zur Vernichtung 'lebensunwerten Lebens', 1890-1945* (Göttingen 1987)

Schneider, Gertrude, *Journey into Terror: Story of the Riga Ghetto* (New York 1979)

Spector, Shmuel, *The Holocaust of Volhynian Jews, 1941-1944* (Jerusalem 1990)

Steinbacher, Sybille, *'Musterstadt' Auschwitz. Germanisierungspolitik und Judenmord in Ostoberschlesien* (Munich 2000)

Toury, Jacob, 'Die Entstehungsgeschichte des Austreibungsbefehls gegen die Juden der Saarpfalz und Badens (22./23. Oktober 1940 – Camp de Gurs)', in *Jahrbuch des Instituts für Deutsche Geschichte 15* (1986), pp.431-464

Tregenza, Michael, 'Belzec Death Camp', in *WLB 30* (1977), pp.8-25

Weingarten, Ralph, *Die Hilfeleistung der westlichen Welt bei der Endlösung der deutschen Judenfrage. Das 'Intergovernmental Committee on Political Refugees' IGC 1938-1939* (Bern, Frankfurt a. M., Las Vegas 1981)

Wenck, Alexandra-Eileen, *Zwischen Menschenhandel und 'Endlösung'. Das Konzentrationslager Bergen-Belsen* (Paderborn etc. 2000).

Wilhelm, Hans-Heinrich, *Die Einsatzgruppe A der Sicherheitspolizei und des SD 1941/42. Eine exemplarische Studie* (Stuttgart 1981)

Witte, Peter, 'Two Decisions concerning the "Final solution to the Jewish Question": Deportations to Lodz and mass murder in Chelmno', in *HGS 9* (1995), pp.293-317

Yahil, Leni, *The Holocaust: The fate of European Jewry 1932-1945* (New York 1990)

Zuccotti, Susan, *The Holocaust, the French and the Jews* (New York 1993)

INDEX

THE HISTORY OF NAZISM

In-depth studies by leading scholars on the Third Reich covering military history, biography, social history and Holocaust studies.

PUBLISHED

Peter Longerich, *The Unwritten Order: Hitler's Role in the Final Solution*

Perry Biddiscombe, *The Last Nazis: SS Werewolf Guerilla Resistance in Europe 1944-1947*

FORTHCOMING

Martin Kitchen, *Nazi Germany: A Critical Introduction*

Michael Allen, *Hitler's Slave Lords: The Business of Forced Labour in Occupied Europe*

Alfred Mierzejewski, *Hitler's Trains: The German National Railway & the Third Reich*